Uprooted

Uprooted

Sidney Oltman Ferrell

iUniverse, Inc.
New York Lincoln Shanghai

Uprooted

iUniverse, Inc.

For information address:
iUniverse, Inc.
2021 Pine Lake Road, Suite 100
Lincoln, NE 68512
www.iuniverse.com

ISBN: 0-595-30212-2

Printed in the United States of America

For George, who shared the experience with me.
And for Michael and Chris, who came to visit and
learned to appreciate life in the country.

Contents

Finding Home 1

Life After Berkeley. 3

The Red House. 5

Shopping in the Armpit of the World 9

Exile 11

Getting the News 13

Cultural Edges, Culture Shock 15

Choices 17

Reverse Culture Shock 21

Changing Seasons 23

Early Autumn Light 26

September Meadow. 27

Snow Light 28

May Mountain Hike. 29

Adjusting to August 31

The Fourth Season 33

Ghost Trees. 35

Promise of Spring 36

Spring Skiing 38

The Dogs 41

Unwelcome Visitors 43

The Wood Stove 45

Visitors 47

The Commute 49

A Missing Piece of the Culture 53

Listening to the Creek 55

Flowing Water 58

The Creek 61

Stillness 62

Pierrot 65

Gardening with Orange Water 67

Learning the Flora 71

Logging 73

Small Has its Rewards 75

Back Roads Neighbors 77

Fences 79

Lists and Accomplishments 83

New Technologies 85

Repeat Performance 89

Edges 91

Volunteering 93

High Country Spring 95

The Devil's Garden 97

Devil's Garden Reprise 99

Transplanted Wilderness 101

Symbols 105

Strangers in the Night 107

Five Senses on a Summer Afternoon 110

Blackberry Picking 111

Second Guessing Nature, Lament for a Forest 113

Slender Green Strands 117

Fading Green 119

Lost Creek 120

Life Cycle 123

The Comet 125

The Feel of a Place 127

Traces Left Behind 131

Rediscovery 133

The Hike to No Name Lake 135

Winding Up 138

The View From Home 140

About the Author 143

Acknowledgements

In writing this book I owe many thanks to several people. To my family, George, Michael and Christopher, who with love and humor helped me to appreciate the experience of living in the country. To my sister-in-law, Joan Oltman, who inspired me to begin writing through the example of her own literary efforts. To the friends who helped me realize the pleasures of a small community. And to the friend who patiently gave me computer instructions and the encouragement to finish this seven year project.

Finding Home

Feeling at home is something we rarely think of until forced to leave a location for a new place. It came as a shock to face moving from the place where I thought I would live for the rest of my life. With the shock came the realization that I was part of that late twentieth century American social phenomenon, a mobile society following their jobs from one place to another. Being uprooted has become a common occurrence in these times.

As the child of a family who predated and exaggerated the trend of a mobile society, I was actively working on bucking that trend in my adult life. As a young adult I was looking for a place to put down roots. In the eighteen years of my childhood my family lived in five cities on three continents, with a total of eleven moves in the process. In contrast, my husband and I managed to raise our children in one community. A portion of my extended far flung family had also gathered in that area. Our children had grandparents and cousins around them as they were growing up, something I never experienced.

The strong desire to put down roots never disturbed the love of travel I had acquired as a child. Perhaps that nomadic childhood was responsible for a curious attitude which surfaces when I travel. I always look at each place with the question of how it would feel to live there. Having lived in and adjusted to a variety of places and cultures, my imagination easily puts the question before me in each place I visit. But as an adult traveling for pleasure, I was secure in the realization that I would be returning to the place I had made home.

As an adult I had also come to an appreciation and love of wild places. My husband's interest in nature led to a career as a research biologist. By inclination as well as by the demands of the career we were exposed to some of the remote and wild places in the western United States and Canada. Each summer we would move to the mountains of northern California for three months of extended field work. For me and the children it was like having a summer place or going to

1

camp. The secure home, the community we identified with, was waiting to return to at the end of each summer.

In midlife, two thirds of the way through his career, downsizing and reorganization, another phenomenon of late twentieth century American culture, took my husband's job and shook it like a rag doll. He was told he could move two hundred miles north to a research group where his specialty was not represented or leave with a year's pay. Not exactly a vote of confidence, but after all, the organization always comes first.

We felt we had little choice, it was late in a career to start over with another organization. We faced the move with a distinct lack of enthusiasm. Emotionally we were caught unprepared. We were being forced to move from our home, our community, and our family.

We felt exiled, uprooted from chosen ground. But our determined rational minds made all the necessary arrangements. Found a house and land to be a new home, transformed the interior to be a replica of its predecessor, set about exploring the new community. We made new friends. I decided to do some graduate work at a local university, something I probably wouldn't have thought of doing had we remained in the old community. And through it all I got to play out my old traveling game, what would it be like to live here?

Somewhere along the way I began to write about the very different community and life style to which I was adjusting. That process has been both cathartic and educational. Isn't life all a learning experience? I have certainly learned to call two places home. It puts me right in there with the rest of mobile America, adjusting and learning about a new place.

Life After Berkeley

Imagine our dismay when faced with the prospect of moving after twenty eight years in the San Francisco Bay Area. Relatives, friends, careers, our whole community was there. The house we thought we had settled into forever was finally feeling large again after the kids had moved out.

The house had seemed huge to us when we moved in, fresh from cramped university student housing. We had reveled in the pleasure of having an extra room, one with no designated purpose. Adolescence settled that question a few years later with the overwhelming need for private space and freedom from a younger brother. That was about the time the house started to grow smaller, pushed inward by children whose viewpoints progressed from eye level with the kitchen counter to a doorway scraping six feet five. Now we were tripping over legs and feet rather than the stray Tonka truck.

But then came empty rooms again, first one, then another, then one filled again as academic breaks and interim jobs ensued. The pattern shifted and changed but gradually the realization came that there were empty rooms, and the small consolation for that emptiness was space. That space could become the office and finally free the dining room table; the TV might live in one of those rooms and release the living room held hostage to its presence all those years. The house was changing size again, it was growing to fit two people, adjusting to their needs.

Life had settled into comfortable habits. Walks in Tilden Park just a few blocks away. Leisurely weekend perusings in the Shattuck Vine neighborhood. Pleasant hours in the local bookstores. My husband's heart improving fifteen minute bike ride to work. My stimulating interaction with the other members of my weaving studio. A move just wasn't in the picture. Until the 'move or quit the job' dictum came down. Then the picture changed.

Why give it all up? How to give it all up? The Central Valley community where we were to move distinctly lacked culture in our eyes. Rodeo and ranch life were not culture to us. And the summer heat was scorching. We knew that from having spent many summers working in the nearby mountains.

Gradually the thought of the mountains drew us. Wouldn't it be possible to live there on the edge of the valley, escape the summer heat, and even pursue the youthful dream of having some land in the country? The commute shouldn't be bad, it would be thirty miles but with a minimum of traffic compared to molasses-like freeways in the city.

Eventually we found three acres of forest land with a year round creek, a three bedroom house and a barn for the mind-staggering low cost of eighty six thousand dollars. At that price, we could keep the Bay Area house and live in our cabin in the mountains. The city house could be rented out but was so arranged that it would be possible to keep a room and bath for our own use. We would reverse the usual pattern by spending weekends in the city.

And so the move was reluctantly made. I can't say it's been the easiest transition but we are adjusting. I use the present tense because it is an ongoing process. But generally, we've adjusted. We've even been to the rodeo.

The Red House

The house we bought was known by the local realtors as the 'Red House'. It wasn't red on the outside, but inside it was definitely red. Or depending on the room, yellow, or blue. But mostly, it was red. Intense pure colors were the theme and red was the favorite.

We were attracted to the place by the setting. Three acres of tall old forest trees, a curving road across a creek bordered with blackberries, up a small hill to a wooden house among the trees. At first glance we thought the setting so perfect that the house wouldn't matter much. Put in our things and we could make almost any place home. And outside would be that delightful setting.

Then we walked in the door. I think the people were troglodytes. Now cave living is fine. I've always fancied those houses in the Dordogne region of France built into the side of a cliff. Unseen parts of the living quarters extend back into caves in the rock. But I like windows too, and I like looking out of them. And I like light coming into the house. If there is a good view I certainly enjoy being able to see it. The windows in the house were swathed in curtains, three or four layers of curtains, all closed. All right, I could open them, even remove some, cut down the layers. Removing them was the best idea, they were mostly red.

As we began to walk through the house there was a strange feeling of walking on uneven ground. Looking down, I noticed the carpet. Blotchy patches of black, pure red and avocado green swirled across from wall to wall in the two main rooms. Well, it wouldn't show the dirt. Or better still, it could be removed. It would have to be replaced. Not prone to motion sickness, I thought this might be the ultimate test of that tendency if I had to live with that carpet.

Entering the kitchen, the red really hit. All the countertops were red and there were red patterned curtains at the large window, closed of course. There was red and black patterned indoor-outdoor carpeting on the floor and wallpaper with red and yellow figures on the walls. The appliances, thank goodness, were not red, but they were yellow. Not almond, yellow. Mercifully, the cabinets were a natural wood veneer. But dark, cave like.

Next we entered the family room, where I really began to question by ability to stay sane if we bought the house. Or my sanity in making a decision to buy the place. The carpet from the front rooms was there again, and it was everywhere. It was practically the only thing in the room. Three quarters of the space had the floor carved out in a big half circle fronting the fireplace to make a 'conversation pit'. Three steps led down to the pit, the middle one forming a semicircular bench facing the fire. Everything, upper floor, steps, lower floor of the pit, bench and bench back, was covered in the carpet. Black wooden poles at intervals along the back of the bench reached to the ceiling. At least there would be something to hold onto as one swayed through the room, fighting carpet-induced motion sickness. And predictably, the room was dark. The large sliding doors leading to a patio were draped in the requisite red curtains. Even with the curtains drawn the north window let in a minimum of light.

Well, one wouldn't need any furniture in this space. There was an alcove with floor to ceiling shelves for books. Wait a minute! What was I thinking? This room wasn't even a possibility. The bench was uncomfortable, the black poles were like a fence inside the house, the plastic fake wood paneling in the alcove was dark, dark, another recess of the cave. And the pit. The pit with its concrete floor beneath the carpet, encircled by the fence poles rising to the ceiling, felt like nothing so much as a dungeon.

We still had the three bedrooms to see. And we had to walk back through the dungeon room to get out. We almost left, but our curiosity was high. What could they have done to top the rest of the house?

Wallpaper doesn't appeal to me. Especially bold patterns in small spaces. But that's a personal matter, it could be removed. Painted walls could be painted over, and these would need it. There was some visual relief from the red. In the form of blue. Very deep, intense blue. Like being underwater in a cave, like the Blue Grotto. The cave theme again.

And there was yellow. Very bright yellow. The child who lived here must have rebelled against the cave idea. This room at least acknowledged the presence of light in the world. And the curtains were open. For the first time we saw natural light entering the house.

Our tour over, we took our leave, reeling. Finding our land legs, we could hardly wait to get far enough away to exchange comments. There was mutual consensus, the family room remained the jewel in the crown, the masterpiece of kitsch.

We looked at other houses for a month. After two failed bids, we thought we ought to look at the red house again. The lovely setting remained in our minds. Could the house really be as incredibly impossible as we remembered it? It was.

Time was short, we needed to find something. Could we do some basic cosmetic renovations and make the red house livable? We could remove wallpaper, paint the interiors, take down the curtains, replace the carpeting. The kitchen carpeting could stay for a while, at least it didn't show dirt. We'd get to that later. A few more windows would be nice. That could be a job for the next summer. A deck off the front room would be pleasant and give the house a needed transition to the outdoors. Now it was simply an above ground cave plunked down among the trees. That would be a summer job too. The sticking point remained the pit, the dungeon, the whole family room. There was only one thing to do. Tear it out, replace the floor, make it a real room. That would be a one week job at least. And it needed to be done before anything else.

The day the house was officially ours I got the key, drove to the house, opened the door and walked right to a window. I removed the layers of curtains and ripped off a wallpapered plywood box with two pointed arches which had covered the window. Light poured in. Ignoring the carpet, I went into the kitchen where curtains and then wallpaper claimed my immediate attention. Both were down in minutes. More light entered. There was a wonderful view into the trees through the large kitchen window.

On to the bedrooms, walking slit-eyed through the family room in order to see as little as possible. That room was a two person job. We would come with crowbar and hammers tomorrow. By late afternoon I had piles of red curtains and bulging bags of old wallpaper to be thrown away. And I could finally start to see the possibilities. As long as I stayed slit-eyed in the dungeon room.

Shopping in the Armpit of the World

When we told our sons of our impending move from the San Francisco Bay Area to the Central Valley of California, they reacted predictably, each according to his nature. The one who should have been born and raised in the Alaska bush was half jealous, especially after we made the decision to live in the mountains. He knew the area as the dreamscape of a fly fisherman. Our city son, the person who had emerged from all the camping trips and the summers in the mountains favoring mostly the urban part of his upbringing, was appalled. "You've got to be kidding!" he reacted to the name of the town, "It's the armpit of the world!" Half inclined to agree, I tried to mollify things by mentioning our plan to become country dwellers. Inside my head I thought, we'll have to visit him, he won't come to us.

Curiosity and nostalgia did bring him however, armpit or not. Our place in the country became his getaway from the city, as the city would become our retreat. Fly fishing and pure nature-love brought the other one. Not to mention some attachment to family on both their parts.

Once moved, I set out to explore the neighboring town's services in terms of a basic need, food. Thoughts of cattle ranches and rodeos in mind, not to mention the infamous armpit designation, I was pretty sure I wouldn't find what I was used to in the East Bay's 'Gourmet Ghetto'. After all, I had been to a local party in our new community where the Jello salad contained not only marshmallows, but M&Ms as well. I hadn't seen a Jello salad in fifteen years. And never one with M&Ms.

As I expected, I didn't find the foods I had been accustomed to. A good croissant, goat cheese, Peets coffee? Better forget it. Baby artichokes, arugula, any other mushroom than a white button? What are they? And bread. As any San Francisco Bay Arean knows, there is no other bread like Bay Area sourdough. You can give other bread the name sourdough or French bread but it simply is not the same thing. It has no taste, to begin with. The texture is entirely different. It often resembles round balloon bread in taste and texture. The taste and texture all depends on the local yeast and the yeast in the San Francisco area has a unique sourness.

The options were to live without these favorite foods or shop copiously on every trip to the Bay Area. We chose the latter solution, enjoying the added bonus of a wonderfully redolent car interior on each return trip. At the country end there were two or three days of gorging on fresh vegetables and fruits from Monterey Market and newly baked bread from Acme Bakery. For the lean times between, Acme and Vital Vittles bread and Peets coffee do quite nicely when frozen and defrosted on demand.

In the ensuing years, more of the unusual vegetables and fruits have entered the markets here. Goat cheese can be found, but Peets coffee and Acme bread are still unavailable and a true crusty French croissant is unknown. Occasional trips to the Bay Area have consequently been planned around the need for these products, much to the amusement of local acquaintances. But we seem to be unable to live without them, or a least we don't have the desire to. And visiting friends and relatives never need to ask what to bring. Bay Area coffee and bread will always be greatly appreciated.

Exile

Because the move was unchosen, forced if you will,

I've seen the years as a sort of exile,

an uprooting of the mind's home from chosen ground.

The determined rational mind made all the necessary arrangements.

Chose a house to be a home, transformed it to a replica of its predecessor.

The rational mind returned to school, to expand the mind, or mask the sense of

exile.

It made new friends, rewarding but no substitute for old ones.

It went to work, the best tonic for quickly passing time,

filling hours and days with 'things I need to do'.

But every day, below the surface, the unconscious mind nags,

with something that must be said.

'I don't really want to be here', it reminds

in daily mourning for choices lost and contentment left.

Getting the News

When we first moved to the country we didn't give too much thought to getting the news. Perhaps we'd give the local paper a try. It would be a good way to learn more about the immediate community. National television news should round out the picture.

Within days we found we missed the San Francisco Chronicle. We found we could buy it at our local store, a few copies were delivered there each morning. Or it was available in the city where we worked. Home delivery was not an option, the paper would arrive by mail several days after publication. Going a mile up the hill to the local store each morning wasn't easy before we had to leave for work. So we began buying the paper in town and reading it in the evenings. Or saving it to read the next morning at breakfast, a very hard habit to break. So we were always a day behind, reading yesterday's news. Television evening news did make us aware of what we would be reading about the next morning.

We dutifully tried reading the local newspaper for a while. It seemed to take ten minutes to get through the entire thing, cover to cover. A single item of national news might occasionally appear on the front page. It was usually likely to be of a human interest nature rather than something of current political or sociological importance. Any world news was buried somewhere in the interior pages and often no more than a brief paragraph in length. Car crashes, arrests, local pageants and weather stories were the lead articles in most issues. Even announcements of local events were difficult to track down. Pretentiously titled 'The Star Bugle', we soon learned the local nickname, 'The Stark Bungle'. There seemed to be a humorous awareness of its deficiencies even on the local level.

Giving up on the local paper, we now rely solely on the Chronicle. Another aspect of our Bay Area connections we do not seem to be able to shed. Only when really needing information about local events do we purchase the local paper. And each time it is a reconfirmation of why we don't subscribe. Ten minutes after starting to look through it we are wondering why we bothered.

For its part, the Chronicle also lacks something for those readers outside the immediate Bay Area. News from other parts of the state is limited. The Bay Area concept of the geography of the state seems to encompass only the 'City' (San Francisco of course), the surrounding commuter regions, Los Angeles and the South (grudgingly), Sacramento for state government news, and the ski areas of the Sierras. Other geographic areas of the state seem lost or nonexistent, surely not part of California are they? This is particularly evident in the weather predictions. Vast areas of many thousands of square miles are lumped together in vague categories like 'Shasta—Northeast' and 'Sacramento Valley'. Such designations cover areas with elevational and latitudinal changes which make for extreme variety of weather conditions within their assigned boundaries. It's impossible to cover the variety of climates in a one paragraph summary for the whole area.

So why not just rely on local weather sources? Because they seem to take their tips from the same sources as the city papers, assigning predictions to immense areas with even vaguer designations like 'mountains' and 'valley'. Being what I suppose should be called 'foothill' dwellers, we are always left out of this equation. We guess on a combination of the two predictions and are usually surprised by whatever occurs.

Like so many aspects of our rural life, in terms of getting the news we seem to be poised on an edge, grasping bits of information from sources from both parts of our lives, the city and the country. We seem to be unable to let go of old habits.

Cultural Edges, Culture Shock

For years I lived in a city that has an abundance of the qualities of edges. It is near the ocean, it backs up on a drier inland environment, it has edges on both sides. It is also a university town, a classic situation providing social, political, cultural and life style contrasts at every turn. To be a liberal in that town is to be only slightly left of center. Anywhere else you would be a flaming radical. To be a conservative is hardly worth raising your voice for, though in true conservative fashion, some diehards do. A response would be unusual, more likely you would be ignored as simply too incredibly reactionary to be worth a response. But being lovers of discourse, many leftists do respond. At length.

All this leads to a heady mix of ever changing ideas and propositions constantly being examined in the public arena. Living there, one comes to assume a similar rationality in the wider world, a willingness to discuss issues, to revel in new ideas, to examine and come up with workable compromises or newer more exciting alternatives grown out of the original mix. Well. Try living in that wider world. Not just visiting, but moving and living there.

Being reasonably well educated, and having spent many summers in the area we were moving to, I thought I knew what to expect. Still, in the rude shock department I managed to be fairly bowled over. Going to vote for the first time in the new location, I was somewhat surprised by the expressions of wonder when I told the helpers my party of registration. "Democratic? Oh, that'll be in another book." A slimmer book, a book set off to one side I noticed. Okay, I told myself, there aren't many Democrats in this mountain area.

Having signed the book, I was directed to one side of the room with two isolated voting booths with pink curtains. Yes, pink. Across the room, where most everyone else was, were eight to ten white curtained booths. What were the implications of those curtain colors? Were we back in the days of Commie pinko allegations? And why were the booths segregated by party? I was used to a big bank of booths where you took the next empty one, after all it was the ballots that were different according to party. And what would happen to my husband who had recently changed his registration to the Green Party? Would there be a special booth for him with green curtains? Or would they be so flummoxed they wouldn't know what to do with him? Would they send him outside to the woodshed?

I was suddenly acutely aware of my comfortable well-worn Birkenstocks and my eco T-shirt proclaiming support for a Costa Rican biological preserve. I was a distinct contrast to almost everyone there. I was the contrast, but not a natural one. One made unnatural, set aside for observation by others. I was an edge, or over the edge in their eyes, and it wasn't comfortable. But it was humorous, I simply wasn't used to being the edge instead of observing it. But I did have to laugh at myself for being thrown off guard. I had to laugh at finding myself the subject of one of my favorite musings, the intriguing quality of edges. I should accept all this, adapt to being considered an outsider. But unless I'm feeling particularly confrontational, I vote by mail these days.

The Republican ballots are blue. I know because they sent me one by mistake in the last election. They must assume everyone is a Republican. The Democratic ballots are pink, just like the curtains, but I'm the only one who has to see it when I vote by mail.

Choices

Some of the choices, made long before in the heady atmosphere of a university town which valued differentness and options,

I had ceased to remember as choices, they were a part of my persona, as the choice to make them had intended them to be.

No lipstick, no perm or hair dye, no daily makeup, these things said to me, and the rest of the world, that this was who I was.

Acceptance, not advertisement. You could look at me and see the person, not having to go through layers,

Visually peeling off the lipstick, the makeup layers, the hair dye, to get at who this person was.

A thirtyish, fortyish, fiftyish woman with few, some, a lot of gray hairs; I hoped an open face, that welcomed other's differences.

An eye that would meet yours on the street and share a smile or a shrug of incomprehension at some mutually shared occurrence.

Other choices, a good haircut, some nice clothes to round out the wardrobe of jeans and turtlenecks,

The clothes of ethnic or handmade fabrics; made other statements, rounded out, defined the personal choices I had made.

I wondered sometimes if some of the choices had been pure laziness, but preferred to think of them as choices.

With others I basked in the pleasure of all their differences, their statements of who they were.

Youth and accepted age, hippie, yuppie, simple individualist, working class, white collar, Asian, Black, White in myriad variations.

And the strangers among us, sharing their own cultural statements of personality.

A delirious mix of styles and thoughts on any given day. A virtual flowering of choices.

At an otherwise contented fifty, I find myself thrust into a community where differences are unvalued, possibly even unknown and definitely unsafe.

At first everyone looks alike to me, especially those under thirty.

In a uniform of flowered dresses with little lace collars, blown dry hair of medium length and impossible hair spray induced neatness,

Tellers, clerks and waitresses greet you with false cheer.

Their male counterparts in age, whose reversed ball caps are apparently stuck to their heads and impossible to remove,

All seem twinned to pickup trucks whose beds rattle with empty beer cans and plastic oil jugs.

Used to a place where nineteen year olds are students, or taking a year in the 'real world' to 'find themselves',

I am struck amazed by nineteen year old mothers and fathers, children having children.

The sight of children in the daytime is refreshing, I realize I have missed their presence, playing in yards, just being with their mothers at the store.

Daycare and au pairs too often hide them from city viewing, where others see them only on weekend quality-time excursions with their parents.

But the children too wear uniforms, vivid TV and Disney characters emblazon their pants and Tees,

Impressing them with universal personalities sanctioned by the gods of advertising in their tender months.

And my pleasure at child viewing wears thin at the tenth baby sucking a bottle of cola while older siblings clutch candy bars.

The grocery carts are stacked with twelve-packs of soft drinks (sugar-free and diet not withstanding), freezer meals and boxed entrees piled high.

Rarely an orange, apple, or green bean do I see, all is prepacked, ready to eat, save the monstrous packages of beef, destined for the barbecue.

Looking in my cart at bags of fruits and vegetables (limited in variety by my standards) I see I've chosen no prepacked items, there are no cans of soda or beer.

There are no pretty pictures of prepared meals, you need to look at my food to imagine what it will become. It may end up different.

My grocery cart contents are not my only sign of difference, the cause for surreptitious looks,

The Birkenstocks and Guatemalan shirt are definitely out of place, perhaps never before seen by these staring eyes.

Definitely not flowers and lace. Not Tee shirts advertising products.
I feel the looks as an Asian or Black might do, eyes telling them they are out of place.

Truth to tell I see such people rarely, and long to greet them when I do, refreshed by their different presence, missing the mix I was accustomed to.

I stare around at unvaried Whiteness, understanding at last what foreigners claim,

We do all look alike.

Reverse Culture Shock

On monthly return trips to the Bay Area region where I lived for almost thirty years, I experience a kind of reverse culture shock. The real shock has been adjusting to the more conservative rural area where I now live. When I make the return trip to my old haunts the shock is in being aware of what I miss and what I notice.

I accepted diversity as a normal part of the world before I moved. I appreciated it, even reveled in it, and had to adjust to its absence in the new surroundings. It is when I make the return trip that I realize just how much I miss diversity. The mix of people, faces, and clothing, is refreshing, invigorating. In contrast, the sameness in my present location bores and distresses me again as it did with shocking force when I moved.

In the new community everyone looked alike to me at first. Weeks could go by without my seeing a Black or an Asian face. In terms of appearance there seemed to be almost a uniform. People wore the same type of clothing (lots of little lace collars on flowered print dresses) and there was a similarity in hairstyles. To dress differently invited stares.

I found one particular attitude expressed by a style especially amusing. Many young men in the area wore their hair long, in a style which fifteen years ago would have branded one a 'hippie'. Fifteen years back no young man in this rural region would have be caught dead wearing his hair long. My own young sons wore their hair at medium length at that time, reflective of the style popular in the city. When my family came to this area for the summer, the comments about their hair were frequent and often rude and embarrassing to young boys. Now long hair on young men apparently expresses other attitudes in this region. Styles do go round in cycles but those of us old enough can remember when they reflected other lifestyles.

I tend to think of the sameness of appearance as reflecting a sameness in attitudes and opinions. On closer examination, a conversation often proves this observation correct. And there is often an assumption that of course you share the conservative attitudes expressed. As in outward appearances, differences of ideas and opinions are unvalued, seem at times to even be unknown, and are definitely unsafe.

So on return trips to the Bay Area I find myself quite happy to just watch people in all their diversity. The mix of countries, backgrounds, clothing and lifestyles visible on the streets is a heady tonic to one reluctantly becoming accustomed to visual sameness in the population. It's a feast of differences.

Changing Seasons

Before the obvious visual signs that accompany a change of seasons, there are subtle shifts in the smell and feel of the air which announce that a new season is on the way. Though I've always been aware of this, it's become more obvious since living in a rural area. The native earth and forest emit their scents unimpeded by a surrounding grid of pavement and introduced ornamental plants.

When the pervading cold damp air of winter gives way to a day when the very smell of the earth itself is in the early morning air, you can be sure spring is beginning. It may still be cold, the buds on the trees are barely visible as small swellings on the twigs, the wildflowers are still below ground, but that earthy odor speaks of warming and potential growth. The sun will seem warmer that day, the sky somehow bluer.

The first few days of summer may blend imperceptibly with full grown spring. By now the fact of spring is visually well established. Deciduous trees are leafed out, a succession of wildflowers has come, and some have gone, making room for those of summer yet to appear. Still cold spring rains have aided all the early season plant growth. A sure sign of summer is a late rain that draws out the odor of drying, almost dusty earth. The mix of moisture and dry dirt carries a different scent than the smell of spring earth still winter damp that heralded the onset of spring.

The early morning air of the first weeks of summer carries the fruity scent of pine trunks absorbing the first rays of morning sunlight. If you poke your nose into the rifted bark of a big old pine a sweet vanilla smell will reward you. At just the right hour of morning that odor suffuses the still cool air of a soon-to-be warm day. As the heat of summer progresses, you need to arise early to experience the smell. But in the turn of the season from late spring to early summer, it fills the air as an announcement of summer ahead.

As summer bakes to sereness it is perhaps the smell of dried grass and leaves which first makes one think of the coming fall. In coastal California that crisp dry grass smell evokes the gentler fall of that region like nothing else. There September and October, traditional fall months, can be the hottest time of the year. Here in the mountains the smell of drying foliage combines with cooler night air to remind one that really cold weather lies ahead. The earth seems to take longer to warm up each morning. Temperatures at night may be only a few degrees cooler than they were in early August but I find myself describing the night air as cold rather than refreshingly cool. Daytime temperatures still soar into the nineties. I am habituated enough that it no longer seems oppressively hot. But the contrast of a few degrees of lower temperatures at night is noticeable, evidence that things will change in the near future.

The changing light of autumn, that sad light that reminds me the year is waning, is a stronger sign of seasonal change than the steady light change of any other time of year. The slow, hardly noticeable, increasing daylight of each late winter day, the longer cheerful daylight hours of spring and then the glorious bright evenings of summer, I accept with pleasure. If the seasons have a curve, for me winter is the low point, spring an upswing to the joy of summer, fall a downward slope to the following winter's low. The sun's angle mirrors that curve, climbing north to its peak at midsummer, swooping south again with autumn's plunge to the winter solstice. Riding the curve south evokes for me a time of sadness, a melancholia suffuses the softer light rays, the cooler air. The decreasing daylight of each autumn day is a steady reminder of winter ahead. The dying year will not be reborn for long months in this cold mountain region.

The crisp early morning air of autumn doesn't carry the intimate local scents of spring and summer. Now the scents are diffuse, they seem to come from a distance. They are borne by an ever present wind, bringing the feel of far northern places.

By autumn's end the air is more than crisp, it is already cold. My coastal California climate sensibility still resists the mere idea of a cold winter. To my mind this temperature isn't possible, it must be a fluke, a few days of cold which will pass. But it does last. It settles in for the duration of a few months. But the deliciously decadent thing about living in almost any California climate is that a drive of a few miles will take you to a new one. Altitude and the ocean are the keys. Go toward either one and you have yourself a different climate within a matter of miles.

I admit to being utterly spoiled by that possibility. There is delight in sensing the change of a season, the feel and smell of each distinct time of year. There is also infinite relief in being able to leave the sere heat of summer in the valley or the gray slush of melting snow in the mountains for a more temperate alternative. Changing climates in late twentieth century California means climbing in your automobile, not just waiting for the seasons to change naturally. How decadently indulgent, but satisfying.

Early Autumn Light

Softer, smoother, the hard edges gone, assuaging heat, the relief of coolness.

Summer's greens have crisped to brown, late fall's color blaze has yet to be.

The sad light of autumn suffuses the air with melancholia.

The sun's southward curve will plunge into deep winter, bury its warmth in

white drifts.

Sorrowful, early autumn light bends low, sweeping down a slope to winter,

the long quiet season when earth rests.

September Meadow

Crossing a green September meadow, still watered by melting snow,

the earth bounces faintly underfoot.

Fairy heads of waving grasses brush gently against open palms,

feather light and ephemeral.

A rocky water course climbs the slope,

water stilled to silent pools behind each fortress stone.

When no wind blows, the ears cocked for any sound,

the merest trickle can be heard

as liquid streams beneath the gravel connect each tiny pool.

At rest on a log beside an alder choked thicket,

the silent flitting warblers are the only visible movement.

The sky above arcs pure and blue,

all breezes stilled for a moment of intense silence,

a silence you can almost hear.

It makes you want to deeply breathe the clear pure sparkling alpine air,

to soak in the place with eyes and ears and nose,

to take away the essence for later remembering.

Snow Light

Light dry snow falling,

a fine sift of confectioner's sugar drifting down.

When ground and trees are softly covered,

transforming all to curving mounds,

A soft blue glow enters the dark house,

cool, unearthly, bouncing off white walls.

Clouds wrung out, emptied of snow,

gray overcast melts to muted sun.

Sunlight comes from the earth,

fresh fallen snow reflecting sky light.

Always dark, the forest circled house now shines

with reflected light, a rare brightness.

May Mountain Hike

Six weeks too soon the air is hot,

the ground drying to brittle crumbling dust.

No dampened dirt beneath the feet,

no lingering snow banks reluctant to melt,

no whining buzz of infinitesimal snow mosquitoes.

The drying scent of fir and pine needles,

remembered smells forgotten in winter's grip,

propel the memory directly to high summer,

leaping past the damp emerging of mountain spring.

Dry as July, the trail has a packed summer hardness

giving way to the spongy bounce of duff only

as it skirts the shattered slash of wind thrown branches.

Though audible in its down slope canyon,

the stream does not sport its usual spring visibility,

throwing high white spumes of spray.

Only an occasional tree gap glimpse and the cool wafting

of water-chilled air up the canyon slope

are reminders of its presence.

The turning trail leaves even stream murmurs behind,

the sough of high wind in the tall trees,

the circling buzz of an exploring fly,

these are the only sounds,

summer day sounds in mid-May.

Adjusting to August

I live in a region of very hot summers. The heat begins early in June but sometimes even in May there may be a stretch of days down in the valley which are over one hundred degrees. By July that range is pretty much normal. But August is overblown, overripe, unreal, an exaggeration of summer.

At our place halfway up the mountain, the routine ninety degree days of June and July edge up to ninety five, then top the one hundred degree mark in August. This can only mean it is over one hundred and ten in the valley. These are the times when we are reminded why we chose to live at this higher elevation. Why we put up with cold and snow and the occasional need to call the snow plow for our driveway in February. One hundred degrees is possible to deal with, one hundred and ten is off the mark for me.

The August temperatures demand new strategies for keeping the unairconditioned house at a livable level. Homes in our mountain community are not supposed to need air conditioning. August is conveniently forgotten when building houses here. Most are equipped with ceiling fans but not air conditioners or swamp coolers. So we open as many windows as possible after the sun goes down. Close everything during the day. Let the double paned windows do the same job they do in winter, keep the disagreeable temperatures out. It works reasonably well but I miss the proximity of the outdoors.

In summer I like to feel that I'm living outside while I go about my work. It must be those old memories of childhood, spending entire summer days out of doors. I like to feel the breeze and smell the resin from the big pines and firs.

Some of my artwork is actually best done outside. Making handmade paper is a watery, messy job. The cement garage floor cleans up easily after a paper making session and remains a bit cooler for the wetting down. Basketry is easily transportable. Sitting on the cool deck over the creek I have some of the materials right at hand. But I haven't yet figured out how to move my clunky old computer outside. So writing takes place in the usual small secluded corner off the kitchen.

Only my thoughts can be out in the summer air. In my mind I make that air cooler than the August temperatures sizzling outside.

In August the fantasy of outdoor summer living becomes impossible. The windows and doors get closed as the sun rises. The garage is only habitable for an hour or so early each morning despite the liberal splashing of water inherent in the paper making process. Even by the creek there is a pool of still, breathless air. We miss eating dinner outside. But unless we wait until after dark it is an unpleasant experience. So we eat in the darkened dining room with the ceiling fan going full speed. Paper napkins and undressed lettuce leaves can tend to fly around. But the moving air seems cooler than the stagnant atmosphere of the closed up house. We tuck in the napkins like kids and dig into the salads before they can fly away.

Actually I think I prefer the house without an air conditioner. I'm afraid if I had one I would rely on it too much, probably starting in June with the first hot days. I'd seldom go outside to see if it was cooler than I thought. It would never be. We'd seldom eat outside and I wouldn't feel that cool delicious air coming in the windows at night. I'll just have to put up with August. Think of it as super summer, not part of the rest of summer. And when really fed up with it, go higher up the mountain where flowers are just coming into bloom, the breeze blows cool and 'real' summer is still taking place.

The Fourth Season

The move to our ridge top home at 3500 feet put us in an environment where for the first time in our California residence we would be able to experience four distinct seasons. Neither of us had lived through a real winter on a day to day basis since we were children. As adults we had some things to learn about living in the cold and dealing with snow and ice.

I very quickly decided I was glad not to be living in a cold climate with young children. What a lot of work just to get them out the door. The mountains of clothing, soon wet and dirty no doubt. The boots, the mittens, the hats, bad enough that we needed to acquire all this extra clothing for ourselves. Putting on, taking off and cleaning all those cold weather items for little children must take an inordinate amount of time.

Learning to keep the house warm was the first important task in dealing with winter weather. The first year we relied on the wood stove and a fireplace. We tried to avoid using the electric baseboard heaters after the electric bill came for the first month. Well over three hundred dollars for the month, and we had only been using the heaters at the lowest setting. We burned a lot of wood that year. The second year we installed a propane gas wall heater to take over the job of keeping the house at a steady 55 to 60 degrees. When we are home the wood stove heats it up to a comfortable 68. We do wear a lot more clothing inside than we used to in the milder coastal climate where we lived before. A few extra layers of clothing can mean a cord less wood burned over the season. You learn to balance things out.

After a few years of living here I am tired of the reality of snow. But I must admit to still being excited and moved by the beauty of snow as it is falling, transfiguring the landscape. Each time I am entranced with the quality of the light inside the usually dark house during a snowfall. A bluish glow seems to emanate from the white walls. And when the snow stops falling and the sun comes out, the house is brighter than at any other time.

I know now that the beauty of the snow is ephemeral, lasting only as long as I can remain inside looking out. Too soon the concrete pad outside the garage must be cleared, the cars will leave tracks down the long drive to the highway and footprints will make a path out to the barn. Messiness replaces that pristine beauty very rapidly. If I'm lucky to have the time I try to get out the cross country skis and make the first imprints on the new snow be my slender tracks as I circumvent the property, taking in the quiet beauty of the fresh fallen snow.

When our local snowfall has turned to utter mess we are able to hop in the car and drive twenty miles up the mountain where the snow is better for skiing. There are no commercial ski areas in this region but the logging roads and park trails are free and far prettier than a packed groomed trail. I always have the feeling that the few people you meet are there because they really want to be, not because they want to be seen skiing or be with crowds of people. Conversations with fellow skiers are short but friendly. They consist of comments on the snow, how great the skiing is, the beauty of the day. There is no reason to feel competitive or angry that other people are in your way or delaying your chance for a good run. No one is showing off the latest fashionable ski clothing or equipment. Jeans and old jackets are the common attire.

Cross country skiing is a complete physical workout. It leaves you tired but exhilarated. Being able to ski regularly has been one of the benefits of living where we do. A side benefit has been the exercise, but mostly we just thoroughly enjoy being out in the snowy woods.

Though we live where we do get some snow each winter, we are fortunate to be able to drive ten miles down the road and leave it behind. And ten miles in the uphill direction takes us to the realm of real winter. They say California has everything, here it is just ten miles in any direction. Living through winter isn't bad when you know you can drive just a few miles and get away from it.

Ghost Trees

Twenty minutes hard rubber macadam ride to the quiet shush of skis on frosted
snow.

Push, glide, push, glide, the rhythm soothes the week's care in rapid moments.

Misty fog, the horizon surround a small soft edged circle moved forward
by the ski's progress.

Ghost trees appear, vertical lines, crowns lost in misty shrouds.

Snow topped boulders stand sentinel, steaming brown earth at their snow
melting feet.

In snow lined channel the stream runs transparent over its black bed,
colored in celadon froth below small falls.

Tussocks, capped with wind brushed snow, are comical straggling figures in
midstream.

Push, glide, push, glide, the rhythm suffuses all, motion and mind, body and
thought.

A long final glide to macadam's edge, a freeing run to return.

Suffused glow of mind and body ease will carry through return;
ghost trees will march with me.

Promise of Spring

Descending the home ridge, we leave an icy wind,

the last grasp of winter, and enter a new season.

The biting wind transforms to a balmy breeze,

fluttering the foam of new green oak leaves.

The redbud has left its named state

to become a froth of lavender blossoms.

Watchful eyes are rewarded by a swath of color

in lush green meadows.

The rising blooms of cream cups, butter-and-eggs,

lupine and wild onion lift above the sweeping grass in brilliant color.

We trace a tunneled path to river's edge,

a verdant hill slopes left,

to right towers a tangled mass of vine-clothed oaks,

untrodden new birthed grass beneath our steps.

The captured scents bring back every joyous childhood

release from winter's confines.

At streamside we traverse last year's rocky channels,

where water raged in winter storms.

Each smoothed stone is round beneath the foot,

nature's prototype of cobblestone.

A tiny stranded pool is fat with tadpoles,

darting fearfully as we pass,

nosing into new pebble harbors of escape.

Stiff ranks of horsetail, bowing slightly with graceful dip,

cover sandbars reshaped as sun warmed dunes.

The river is swift, leaden hued, heavy with snow melt.

High in its banks, it shows no white fringed riffles

or gray-green shade of a later season.

It is power in a surge to reach somewhere else.

We fill ourselves with spring,

knowing our somewhere else will be

winter on the mountain still.

But we have felt the promise.

Spring Skiing

My skis glide at the meeting place of the sky's bright blue bowl

and crisp mounds of a full winter's snow.

A six foot snow pack lifts me skyward,

at bird's eye level with tree trunks,

reaching for the blue bowl above.

Across the valley two free spirits have left

perfect parallel serpentine tracks down the crater's face,

leaving no trace of how they gained the top.

Buried by December storms, small trees spiral skyward

each in its own tunnel of spring melting snow.

Tiny snow craters display a single pine cone,

or a yellow green spray of staghorn lichen.

I reach a meadow with meandering stream

where softly rounded untracked mounds

cleave for the passage of the creek's clear flow.

At rest, drinking in the day, the silence is complete,

the birds have flown to lower spring visited slopes.

In motion, I try to decide which I prefer,

the shush of skis over crystaled snow

and the companionable plop and hiss of poles,

Or the cool zephyr of air that hangs above the snow,

cooling my face on a warm sunlit spring day.

The Dogs

My biologist husband somehow successfully resisted our young sons' pleas for a dog until the younger son turned eleven. We got an intelligent, pretty, Heinz 57 variety puppy from some friends when their dog produced a litter of eleven. In addition to her other qualities she was to prove long-lived. She held out until she was sixteen. Of course her favorite person was the one who had resisted getting her for so long.

Not to be outdone by his younger brother, our older son bought himself a Black Lab pup when he was nineteen. Jess went off to college with his master at four months of age. That lasted one strained semester, then Jess lived with us. This all took some adjustment on the part of Shasta, who definitely considered herself the queen of the household. An aloof sniff was about all she wanted to give the rambunctious young rascal who had invaded her six year reign.

Shasta did not go off to college with her master, her queendom was too well established. The adults in the picture had fallen into an old trap, the kids left, the dogs didn't. We asked ourselves why we hadn't just gone through the process when the boys were younger, then the dogs would have been out of the picture by now. We did admit, grudgingly, to a growing affection for them however. They were definitely part of our lives. We were trapped.

When the need to move came, there was some thought in our minds that the dogs would appreciate having room to roam. Our ultimate choice of place was not a little dog influenced. The dogs joined us on our explorations in the country around our new home. There were more excursions than we managed in the East Bay because outdoor activities were closer to hand. The dogs were quite happy with the situation.

Cross country skiing, which we usually managed only once or twice a winter, was now just twenty minutes up the highway. Or right out the door on occasion. If the snow wasn't too deep we'd take the dogs along for a good workout. We thought they would follow in the tracks we made; it seemed reasonable. Jess's

41

personality being what it was, eagerness personified, we should have remembered that he'd want to be out in front leading the way. No sedate following in some-one else's tracks. He surged ahead through a foot of snow, his barrel chest shed-ding snow like a plow. Shasta trotted nimbly behind, her slight build preventing her slim feet from sinking through the crust. This was the dog who made us won-der if cross species breeding weren't possible. She could leap to the top of a six foot fence, pivot on its six inch wide top and walk along to a suitable jumping off spot to escape the confines of our city yard. She was very cat-like at such times.

In summer the dogs accompanied us on four or five mile hikes in the nearby wil-derness areas. Jess would roam far ahead or out to one side as wing scout, return-ing occasionally to check our progress. We were never sure how he knew our destination but he usually met us there with a "where have you been" look. If he wasn't waiting a whistle would bring him crashing through the undergrowth, already having surveyed the whole area. We figured he usually did about three miles to each of ours. The five mile hikes were more like fifteen for him.

Timid by nature, Shasta stayed closer and if she did range ahead on the trail, she would return frequently to make sure we were coming. With advancing age she was getting deafer and this was probably a wise tactic on her part.

The dogs would return home exhausted, we merely exhilarated, by the exercise. Poor Jess suffered from hip problems common to many Labs and was often in some misery for a day or two. There seemed to be no way to slow him down and remind him of the consequences of too much running. He would lie immobile on the rug and seemed to appreciate my ministrations with a heating pad applied to his hips. Or maybe he just liked the extra attention. The vet told us that aspi-rin would help too. We dosed him as soon as we got home.

But all the extra pleasure of excursions aside, the dogs were quite happy just roaming our land and the nearby woods. In fact they were delirious with pleasure in their new environment. They romped over our three acres chasing gray squir-rels, digging holes anywhere they wanted without reprimands, cooled off in the creek, and generally told us in a thousand ways that dogs were meant to live in such a place.

Unwelcome Visitors

Having moved to a new community we became subject once more to the visits of a certain religious group. In our previous community we had finally become know to them as unfertile ground. It was annoying to have to go through it all again. They always took a lot of convincing.

We always felt doubly put upon when they came to our door because we had also had to deal with their pressure on a personal level when a family member joined their ranks. At a needy time in her life she fell for their reassuring manner and determined sureness of their own correct ideas. Fine for her, we even eventually accepted the rightness of it for her. But the rider was that it did not end with her. Pressure was put upon her to bring in her entire family. She was told that without that action on her part some of the promises would not even work for her.

A trying period ensued where we were trapped into accepting surprise visits from her with 'friends' in tow. The friends always turned out to be the strongest of the proselytizers. My biologist husband at first enjoyed the repartee of a lively debate on evolution. The 'debates' soon became more like battles, there was no give and take on one side of the issue. Eventually a brave soul took pity on our relative's miserable inability to sway any of her family. Somehow she must accept that she would not see us in Heaven. The word went out to lay off the pressure on her recalcitrant family. We were vastly relieved. We had always wondered about that space in Heaven anyway. The one hundred forty four thousand figure for those who would enter Heaven was less than their worldwide membership. There was going to be infighting for those spots sometime.

The nameless group began sending out proselytizers within days of our arrival at our new house. Enough to make you wonder if they didn't after all have some link to a Being knowledgeable about the moves and locations of all humans.

At home more often than my husband, I was the one who usually got the visitors. My first approach was to be polite, telling them I had my own beliefs. Failing that (according to them their beliefs were always better, and right), I tried arguing.

That was hopeless. I tried telling them we had a relative who was a member so we knew all about it. "Well, then why hadn't we joined?" It did save me having to buy their literature, I told them we could get it from her. We did. Occasionally.

Sometimes I saw their car coming up the drive, always an older make of an American model, and I could tell who it was. Heartlessly I would let our rambunctious dogs out to circle their car, barking menacingly. They would stay in the car, shouting to me. I feigned deafness or helplessness with such unruly dogs.

My final tactic was to simply retreat to the back of the house if I was lucky enough to spot them coming. I simply didn't answer the doorbell and sat out the time reading a book in the bedroom. Little gifts of literature would be left at the door, making me feel guilty and impolite.

All my methods seemed to end up making me feel somehow at fault. No doubt they had training to achieve that result in those they confronted. The method I hated most was when they brought the children along to practice proselytizing. You have to listen to an earnest little child. I should have remembered the way my dad had once handled one of their visits. I think it is the best approach I've heard of.

Busy one afternoon cleaning the ashes out of our old coal burning furnace, he was surprised outside the house by a group from the same religious sect. When they catch you outside you have to talk to them. He listened politely, talked to them but never mentioned his own affiliation with another church or that he was actually employed by a church organization. After some fifteen or twenty minutes of persuasive talk, one of them asked him, "Mr. Oltman, are you ready to accept Jesus Christ here in your home tonight?" Dad answered equally politely. "No, not tonight. I'm pretty busy right now. And we're expecting other people over tonight." They left without retort.

Our own unwelcome visitors took longer to convince of our unwillingness to join them. Eventually I think they just got tired of no one answering the door.

The Wood Stove

In winter I feel like the wood stove controls my life. It requires four armloads from the woodpile each morning to keep it stoked for the day. And it's not just a dash out to the woodpile to collect the needed fuel. I need to 'suit up' in boots, jacket, hat and gloves to survive four trips out into the cold.

If I'm feeling historical, each load is a pioneering push back of the surrounding wilderness, asserting my family's right to be here, establishing our hold on this place. In literary mood, and slightly more frantic, my mind's eye has me in the far cold north helping Jack London's freezing man build a campfire.

I've learned to build a good quick fast burning fire that raises the interior temperature by a few heart warming degrees within an hour. Four sticks of cedar kindling in a rack, topped with a couple of split cedar logs. When it has become a glowing pile, add a couple logs of dense oak or alder which will burn slowly and keep the heat coming. A few years ago I would have had no interest in that information, now it's crucial. And it cuts down my slavery to the iron monster, I only need to check it every few hours to see if I need to add more fuel.

A clear sunbright winter day. Drifts of dry snow pellets lie frozen and unmelting until mid-afternoon. The temperature finally breaks the freezing mark about one in the afternoon. Struggling from the warm cloud of down comforter above and featherbed below at the usual weekday early hour, we had faced the fact that the inside temperature had dropped to fifty five again. Arriving home late last night after a weekend in warmer climes, an immediate fire brought it up to sixty before we sought the warmth of the duck down. But during the night the temperature had dropped back down to the 55 degree level.

The morning temperature reading meant there was a day ahead of feeding the stove in hopes of reaching a livable sixty eight degrees by evening. Better plan to stay home for the day or we'd be two steps forward and one backward in the temperature department. The very walls would have to be heated up. Four trips to the woodpile and hourly stoking got the temperature up to sixty two by two o'clock. It goes faster with more bodies moving around the house, but this is a one person task today, my husband is off to the warmth of a centrally heated office.

Historical or literary, I have my choice of moods. But the iron monster rules today. I think a musical mood is most fitting, you load sixteen tons and what do you get, one degree warmer, and not done yet.

Visitors

Sometimes my husband and I say to each other that we don't really know where we live. We are on the road so often, three days there, four days here, two in another place, that it becomes difficult to know which bed is the one we long for the most at the end of a long hard day. Essentially we live in a northern California rural area near a sizeable valley city. But there is also our house in the Bay Area, our actual home for twenty five years and our minds' home still. We still visit there on a regular basis.

Then there is my husband's work as a biologist whose job is field research. Northern California is his laboratory. During six months of the year he moves around a lot. Checking experiments, reviewing new sites, responding to requests for information from other field biologists. Whenever possible, if not occupied with my own design business, I enjoy accompanying him as his number one volunteer.

There was always that dichotomy in our lives, the high pleasure in the less populated parts of the state and the comforting return to the home base. In our case that base just happened to be one of the more stimulating places to live in California, and quite the political and philosophical opposite of the rural areas we loved to visit. We became quite nimble in our leaps from one of these edges to the other.

A few years ago my husband was presented with the option of moving his base of operations to a more rural area, or of leaving the organization. Too young to think of retirement, we opted on the side of economic necessity, the need for a continued income, and reluctantly made the move.

The change was not made without a considerable amount of agonizing. In this we had the support and sympathy of many friends and relatives, all of whom could not imagine moving from the stimulation of the cosmopolitan area we all loved in a way which was more than its simply being our home. They watched our plans and the move with interest, all promising to be visitors in the near future. When we chose to live in the mountains, thirty miles from the city where the new office would be, that increased the desire of many to see our new place. Everyone, including us, had a bit of that desire for a place in the country.

We played off their curiosity to assuage our early loneliness in the new community. We hosted house parties for large groups of friends and relatives. They arrived eager to see what life in the country was like. And to see if people from the rarified air of the East Bay could make a go of it in such a different setting.

They arrived with emergency supplies of Acme bread and Peets coffee, things they knew we couldn't live without. We took them fishing or cross country skiing; both possible within a twenty minute drive of our new house. In the spring and early summer we went on wildflower hikes to see things they usually saw only as fleeting glimpses from a car window.

Some were even willing to rake pine needles and chop wood, chores we'd quickly learned were endless, not a novel aspect of country life. Their help was appreciated although we knew we'd be back at it again as soon as they left. And they usually tended to burn up all the wood they chopped, heaping logs on the fire in wasteful abandon. We'd learned very quickly how many logs were needed to raise the temperature to a livable level without the help of a mechanical thermostat to tell us it was comfortable. We'd also learned to pile on more clothes rather than more logs on the fire to raise our personal temperatures.

Everyone made return visits, some even came on a yearly visit at a particular time of year. But gradually the interest has tapered off. They know we survived. And they can see us on our monthly jaunts to the Bay Area. And two hundred twenty miles each way is a long way to travel for a weekend. Don't we know it.

We seem to find ourselves making that journey every third or fourth week. Sometimes we don't know where we live. Just somewhere in northern California. Or maybe our real home is on Interstate 5.

The Commute

My daily commute covers thirty miles and three thousand feet in elevation change each way. From the five hundred foot valley floor to our 3500 foot ridge I pass through several life zones, often as many microclimates, and frequently an equal number of mood changes. The temperature changes as well, getting hotter as I descend the ridge in the morning and cooler by ten or twenty degrees as I climb the ridge in the afternoon.

Going down in the mornings, particularly in summer when the valley can reach a hundred and fifteen degrees and averages one hundred for six weeks in midsummer, I frequently ask myself why I am going to spend the day in a place that can get so incredibly hot. Then my thoughts turn toward the work day ahead and there is little time to notice the landscape change as I descend the ridge.

The day is spent in an air conditioned space, an artificial setting which can annoy me if I think about it. The comfort it provides doesn't annoy me, there is really no desire to be out in the heat, but the very necessity of it. I prefer to be a part of the natural setting, to go outside occasionally and sense the day's weather if I can't spend the day outside. At one hundred degrees and above my desire to commune with nature diminishes rapidly. I give in to the artificial environment, even putting on a sweater in the overly cool office, to concentrate on the work.

Toward the end of the work period I allow some thoughts of home to creep into my brain. A forty minute commute will be necessary in order to attain the cooler temperatures, the visual greenness, the balmier breeze. Maybe I even appreciate those things more for having to go through the commute. The daily contrast of the two environments makes me more acutely aware of the benefits of the home site. And the drive gives me a chance to acclimatize, to anticipate and to appreciate the transitions.

The dash from the air conditioned building to the not yet air conditioned car is enervating. Like opening the door of a blast furnace, the dry heat can take your breath away. It takes determination to enter the baking interior of the car. As the air conditioning kicks in after a few minutes relaxation is at last possible. I can begin to take note of the passing landscape.

The valley floor is baked and dried out by early summer, I am glad to leave it behind. Heat waves shimmer off the ground, whether dry red dirt or thinly covered with toasted golden grasses. Sparse to begin with, the native vegetation has been largely cleared where development has taken place. Builders seem to rely totally on the machinery of air conditioning, not realizing the cooling propensity of trees around a building. Not to mention the visually soothing properties of green foliage. It is another artificial aspect of modern life which annoys me. And one of the reasons we chose to live where development has not run roughshod over the landscape.

The intensity of development diminishes just where the road rises into the first hills. It is also just where the road begins to dip and curve, something it will do for the next twenty miles until it reaches the long ridge top. This hill country is beautiful in the spring, rolling expanses of grass and wildflowers interspersed with blue oak groves. The unrelenting heat and continual sunshine of summer sere it quickly. At this time of year it is a place to be driven through, there is no desire to stop.

As the hills rise to the lower ridges gray pines and scrub oak struggle to keep a flush of green during the long months when grasses and brush have turned tinder dry. This is a region of thin rocky soil and seasonal surface water; all the running water lies deep in side canyons. When we first moved here I labeled this area 'the wasteland'. A bit harsh I now realize but for me its only beauty is in spring. It is still an area largely without human habitation, water and shade being at a minimum.

At two thousand feet the mixed oak and conifer forest begins. Visually there is more variety in the vegetation and green takes over from the predominant dry gold of the lower grasslands and scrub oak plateau. Forested areas are now interspersed with homesteads, usually houses on several acres, well spaced from each other.

Despite its length it is not a bad commute. Traffic is moderate and rarely do you encounter the speeding motorist who must be the first on the road. Most drivers seem to be enjoying the ride. Even the slow trucks and RVs laboring up the long slope are taken with equanimity by most drivers. With few places to pass, everyone seems to realize they might as well settle back and look around a bit. It gives one a chance to notice things one doesn't see when hurrying down the hill to work. The vegetables coming up in the small truck garden farm, the flowers blooming in someone's yard, the white lupines and wild grape taking hold on the road cut just below my drive; I wouldn't notice these at all if I were driving fast.

When I reach my property the long driveway enters my woods, crosses the small babbling creek and winds up the hill to the house, filtering out the highway, the traffic, the day in the town, the heat. Shaded by tall trees, the house is cool without benefit of an air conditioner. A walk around the property to check on the latest wildflowers, the trout in the creek and the state of the vegetable garden is sufficient reward for the thirty mile commute. I'll do it again tomorrow just for the pleasure of coming back.

A Missing Piece of the Culture

There's a whole piece of American culture I've been missing. I knew it, but I've just been reminded of it again. I've been traveling, staying in motels with televisions that have access to a great variety of channels. I don't normally watch commercial TV. I find that I have very little patience with commercial breaks. The time allotted for advertising breaks seems to almost equal the time of the actual program. Just as one begins to concentrate on the story, there is a commercial break with three or four jarring advertisements. I simply don't want to put up with the interruptions.

At our house we can only get two channels on the television. One is a major network channel, the other, thank goodness, is a public educational station. Of course if we were to invest in a satellite dish, as many of our neighbors have, we could receive more stations than we could ever hope to watch. There are too many books I want to read, too much music to listen to, too many projects to do, to spend time surfing those channels. Much less putting up with the commercials on most of them. So selected programs on the educational station are about the only TV seen in our house.

As a result, I often have no idea what people are talking about when they refer to current commercials or sitcoms they have watched on TV. As in, "did you see that commercial for cars?", or phones, or soap, or whatever. The cleverness of the latest masterpiece of the ad world is lost on me. Doubly. I don't know about the product and I don't appreciate the wit of the newest commercial.

I'm equally at a loss when the plots or characters of the latest sitcoms are discussed. People talk about the characters on TV as if they were their friends or neighbors. At first I think I am participating in a conversation about someone they all know well. When I realize the talk is about a TV program the discussion soon flows past me, over my head. I tend to regard these situations the way I regard my friend who goes on endlessly about the personal lives of her co-workers. A few minutes of gossipy detail about the domestic affairs of people I don't know and I'm afraid my eyes glaze over. I have the same reaction to the complete rehash of last night's TV program. In the end they are both something we have no control over. No input on our part will affect next week's program, no thoughts from me to my friend will reach her co-workers. I can offer no comments or input in either case.

But I do realize there is a whole slice of the culture I'm missing. The programs on TV provide a new binding between people who watch them. They provide a shared experience. It's something I've simply chosen not to share. But when I travel, I do take the opportunity to sneak a look at some of the current shows. Just so I'll know what people are talking about. The ads though are more than I can take. I still mute the sound during the commercial breaks. I guess I just don't mind being thought of as a know-nothing during the conversations about commercials. But I sure would like to discuss the latest book I've been reading.

Listening to the Creek

One of the first projects we tackled on our new property was to build a deck over the creek. Technically it is a bridge, it lets you walk, but not drive, from one side to the other. But chiefly, it was built for contemplation. It replaced a narrow tumbled down log structure, possibly built for the same purpose but only wide enough for walking.

Our grown sons came to our new home for Christmas that first year just after we had made the move. As it was not their home territory, they knew no one but us and were eager to have something to keep them busy. We set them to building the deck over the creek. On Christmas Eve they felled two small cedars to serve as supports, somehow wrestling each eight inch diameter log across the stream. On Christmas day they secured the structure with a deck of 2 x 4 boards, taking a break for turkey and stuffing.

It was a mild winter but not warm enough to let us celebrate with a meal on the new bridge. We'd have to wait for summer for that pleasure. The boys were motivated though to find a way to stay outside near the water. They built a sweat lodge of branches beside the creek, covering the sides with black plastic and banked pine needles. Eager for a full experience, they built a small fire inside, heating up rocks which they planned to douse with creek water to create steam. They shivered through an hour or so of precise preparations. Preferring a snug house on a winter evening, we awaited the retelling of the experience inside. When they entered not rosy and invigorated but simply cold, we knew the experiment was not a complete success. But it was an initiation of future creek side rituals.

With the passing of several years, the bridge has become a favorite spot on hot summer days. I try to find at least an hour each afternoon to spend there quietly absorbing the surroundings. Mostly I listen to what the creek has to say. Starting with the sounds of water, I gradually take in the streamside environment.

The sounds created by the path of the water make a music sufficient to drown the noise of passing cars on the road. And the creek flows in a slight hollow, shutting out the sight of civilization as well. Upstream from the deck, the water tumbles over rounded stones, with several slides and tiny frothing falls for variety. The bridge sits at the base of one of these little falls, at the start of a long pool. There, beneath a cut bank below a leaning cedar, live our resident rainbow trout. We have seen as many as four at one time, usually there are one or two. It takes a bit of persistence to see them. The clear water is a window to the tea colored silty bottom where the trout lie undulating in the current. Sitting quietly for five or ten minutes puts them at ease to resume their underwater grazing. I like to think they accept me as part of the setting as I sit motionless above their pool.

Shifting my glance to the surface of the water I take in the quick flashes of busy blue darters. A delicate spider hovers in mid air above the falls by the deck, her web invisible except at just the right angle to a shaft of sunlight. A gently nodding reed on one bank reveals one anchor of the web, a bent lily stalk secures the opposite side. In a slow shallow bay of the trout pool a monstrous black and gold dragonfly taps the surface film with her tail, repeatedly seeking the perfect spot for laying her eggs. Perhaps her generous deposits will provide the trout a meal as well as insure the survival of some of her progeny.

In June and July the creek banks are lined with tall gracefully dipping orange leopard lilies and a sprinkling of red and yellow columbines. Often swallowtail butterflies can be seen visiting each open flower in turn, making purposeful treks up and down the banks.

Forming a shaded tunnel down the stream, alders sink their roots as close to the water as possible. Cedars like the waterside as well, some of them curving a graceful swell out over the water before soaring skyward. Oaks and firs stand back behind, adding to the greenly shaded glade. Under the cool shade grow a profusion of blackberries.

On even the hottest days a gentle breeze wanders down the waterway. Even this merest suggestion of air movement can be refreshing. Added to the sound of running water, its cooling propensities seem to be enhanced.

The deck has become a place where I go to feel and watch a small natural world. It is a place for reconnecting with nature. Through all these observations the background chorus of the water is ever present, its music enhancing the visual pleasures. I need to listen to the creek as often as possible.

Flowing Water

By the laws of humans I'm allowed to call the creek my own.

It flows across my property at the base of a rolling hill.

But by all the laws of nature I can never call this moving water mine.

Free, flowing, each water drop visits

my two hundred feet of land for no more than a few minutes.

The creek bed? Maybe that I can call mine.

But the water constantly shapes it, the water is in control.

Water scours and cuts the bed,

scoops and undercuts the banks,

making homes for darting trout,

leaving trees at crazy overhanging angles.

Two bridges cross the stream, by rights they are mine,

part of the manmade world imposed on the creek.

One I drive over to reach the house,

a connection to the world of civilization, people and machines.

The other bridge rests lightly on opposite creek banks,

its log supports cut from trees once rooted on its shores.

Its open deck is meant for contemplative musing

above the flowing stream,

a place to absorb sounds and smells,

and the sight of darting dragonflies.

Water sounds mask the roar of cars and grind of uphill trucks,

shutting out manmade noise.

This bridge will only bear a walker,

or a dreamer wishing to greet the water

as it visits briefly the land I call mine.

The Creek

We saw four trout in our creek a few weeks ago. The largest was about sixteen inches long. They held steady below a cut bank under a large leaning cedar. We stealthily watched from our bridge-to-nowhere, the deck we built across the stream for catching the cool air flow and for creek watching.

There were no fish visible in our yard wide creek when we built the deck. To our surprise and delight the darting shape of a six inch trout appeared late the next summer. A fluke we said, washed down from the lake above. But it stayed and was joined by others, all about the same stunted half foot size.

The four large ones were a complete surprise. We had assumed the stream would only support the six inch variety. But storms and weather have changed the creek. A flash flood one spring scoured out the bed and made it more of a sluice than a meander. A heavy fall freshet took the bed down another few inches and carved the cut banks deeper, creating several adjacent deep pools.

Accompanying the flash flood, a good deal of our upstream neighbor's LA Urban Dream Farm was washed down and caught amongst our bank side blackberry patches. Perhaps the bags of chicken feed and rabbit pellets left nutritious deposits in the shallows and backwaters, luring the larger trout to new waters. There was much else left by that rage of water which would not have enticed fish. But several days of booted wading and bramble caught legs in the blackberries removed the shreds of plastic, twisted corrugated tin roofs of former chicken coops and odd pieces of nail studded timber. The stream's renewal to trout-enticing waters took place over the next nine or ten months.

We watch regularly for the four new fish but do not always find them beneath the cut bank where we first spotted them. We fear each new storm will change the creek again. But perhaps the trout are cruising in pools above or below the bridge-to-nowhere and will return some time to let us spy them again. We keep a sharp lookout.

Stillness

A diffuse mellow golden light wraps earth and sky,

binding the two in stillness.

Even the sounds are quiet, the low rustle of falling leaves,

the plop and bounce of plump acorns dropping

to hide in crisp curling leaf mounds.

The soft rat-tat of industrious woodpeckers

storing food for winter.

Only an occasional raucous cry,

as perceived invaders fly too close,

bespeaks the urgency of seasonal change.

Gurgling faintly, the swift smooth

flowing creek is barely audible.

A clear dark band in the toasted golden landscape,

it runs unruffled over a clear chalk bottom,

swathed with undulations of green-black weed beds

where dark trout lie waiting to surge

to the surface for an ephemeral mayfly.

Combed green tresses lie sweeping the sandy bottom,

curling tendrils breaking free

to float away on the smooth current.

Miniature eddies dot the water's cool surface,

tiny jets of frivolous energy spinning round

fragile leaf boats launched upstream.

Growing has ceased, restful release of summer's

budding energy stills each grass and tree.

No breath of wind alters the hush of a world

waiting for winter solitude.

Rest, before spring demands

the energy of regrowth.

Pierrot

Pierrot came visiting today, making the rounds of our property. He dug under the cyclone fence around our neighbor's LA Urban Dream Farm to visit our greener pastures. Pierrot is our neighbor's piebald black and white rabbit who has fattened on our flowers for the past three years.

Before Pierrot and assorted cousins began their visits we tried to grow a few flowers around our house. Mostly our gardening has consisted of appreciating the wildflowers, reducing the fire danger by removing brush and small trees, and cutting some medium sized trees for firewood. But a longing for the wildflowers to last a bit beyond early spring, and nostalgia for things like cosmos, penstemon, aquilegia and Shasta daisies led us to put in a small flower patch near the house.

Pierrot and a companion began to appear quite regularly at a grassy area down near the highway. Graze, whose name derives both from his hazy color and from his eating habits, usually stayed in the meadow area below. But Pierrot was bolder and soon he had crossed the bridge over the creek and began appearing up near the house. He was fearless. He hung out under our parked cars and did not flinch at our approach.

We observed Pierrot munching on the one wildflower we disliked, the omnipresent meadow rue. In the fall it forms very sharp sticky seeds which lodge easily on any part of you or your clothing, poking sharply. Pierrot seemed to like the meadow rue. We didn't, so we put up with his presence near the house since we thought he was reducing the amount of the hated rue.

In the back of my mind I feared for the flowers we had planted. But for some time he was occupied with the meadow rue. There was lots to occupy him. Each day I looked to see if any flowers had been sampled. So far so good for the first few weeks.

The inevitable happened. He eventually found the flowers. Or finished the available meadow rue. He didn't finish the flowers off all at once. But eventually all but the penstemon were nibbled down to ground level. We waited for the penstemon to go. Was it being saved for dessert? But it stayed. Pierrot went off to new pastures. He apparently didn't like it. We had one flower we could plant. Later flower beds have consisted solely of penstemon. Visual boredom was somewhat alleviated by planting every color available. Still, each garden was all penstemon. Occasional attempts to see if Pierrot had forgotten his taste for aquilegia or cosmos always proved the constancy of his food tastes, they were mowed down within days.

One day in spring I was curious about the scrabbling sounds under a low deck off the living room. I quietly watched as three baby rabbits ventured out to sun themselves. Pierrot also hung around watching. Prompting me to wonder if he was misnamed. Should he/she be called Pierrette? Despite annoyance over the flowers, I seemed unable to resist giving all the babies names. The pure black baby and its mixed color siblings became Inka, Dinka and Doo.

The babies did not reside long with us, apparently preferring the safety of the chain link fence around the LA Urban Dream Farm. Graze is an occasional visitor, when the grass is lush and green. Pierrot, the bold adventurer, spends the most time with us. This despite, or perhaps because of, the fact that a mountain lion has visited the Dream Farm. A dog and a large goat both suffered the indignity of its claws along their bellies. Perhaps Pierrot is safer among the blackberries and manzanita thickets outside the chain link fence.

Gardening with Orange Water

I've always wished I had a green thumb. I'm finally beginning to admit that I don't, but I can't seem to stop trying to prove myself wrong. I continue to have fantasies about lush vegetable gardens and bountiful flower borders. Admitting the probable impossibility of either of those fantasies given my gardening skills, I'd settle for living in a field of wildflowers. Probably that's also a fantasy.

When we moved to three acres in a rural area a few years ago, the faded fantasies leapt to the front of my consciousness once more. Was it possible they might finally be realized? We would have the space, the land on which to try again, maybe this time the fantasies would prove real. What I was conveniently ignoring was the nature of the soil, the presence of a forest of shade trees, and the type of water our new well produced. This was the sort of information which had always defeated me as a gardener in the past. I always looked at the end product and never understood the growing process. If I bought small plants well started in one inch pots (I had long ago given up on trying to grow anything from seed), watered and weeded them attentively, why shouldn't I end up with lush vegetation like that splashed across the pages of home magazines in gorgeous full color photographs?

The first spring after our move we looked for the best garden site. Our new property had a barn with an adjacent fenced area which the previous owners had used as a pig run. It was the spot most open to sun on the entire forested plot. There was water at the nearby corner of the barn. Though the pig run now sported a crop of seedlings from a huge overhanging incense cedar, we thought the soil might contain a residue of pig droppings which would act as fertilizer. And knowing the rooting habits of pigs, we thought perhaps their activity might have loosened the hard volcanic soil. What dreamers we were.

Both those things may have happened, but we came to realize that the period of residence of the pigs must have been some time ago. Once we got to working the soil, there was little evidence of the beneficial efforts of those creatures. The stony red volcanic soil was a far cry from the rich loamy black soil of a gardener's dreams. Even our six months effort at making a compost pile had not produced enough to add much nourishment to that sterile ground.

Undaunted, we rented a rototiller at the nearest rental place twenty miles away. We loaded it in the back of our Isuzu Trooper (which was surely not designed for holding such items) and laboriously unloaded it at our garden site by means of portable metal ramps. Overly ambitious, after all, we had the space, we tilled a twelve by thirty five foot area. After much raking and a good deal of hand sifting we disposed of many of the larger rocks. We chose to ignore the smaller rocks well sprinkled through the soil. We added our available compost mixed with straw and old chicken manure which we had gotten from the floor of the barn. The completed plot actually looked like it would grow things, why not try seeds?

The next order of business was hooking up a watering system. A long hose leading to a moving sprinkler head and an automatic timer did the trick. The water to the barn came straight off the well and did not run through the complicated rust removal filter system for the house water. We knew that the iron in the water left a rusty residue. When we tried the new system, a bright spray of orange water emerged from the sprinkler. A bad omen. But that was overshadowed by our delight in having put in a real garden.

Almost daily checking revealed tiny plants actually emerging, from seed! Of course there were bare patches, not nice even rows of emerging green, but it was better than the nothingness of past seeding attempts in other gardens. The water, orange or not, was working its miracle, encouraging growth.

About the third week after planting I noticed one day that part of the garden was dry after a watering cycle. The sprinkler had not been rotating as it should. Checking it over, I noticed bright orange deposits of muddy rust in many of the holes along the rotating shaft. A simple ream out with a pin to each of the eighteen holes along the shaft and a readjustment and scraping of the rotation gear corrected the problem. But I realized this would no doubt be an ongoing chore. In addition the leaves of some of the larger plants we had put in were beginning to show a rusty film. Lush greenness was not going to be a part of this garden.

The first year's garden, while not lush by any standards, produced enough to make us think of doing it again the next year. There were, of course, some total failures. No carrots came up at all, the corn never bore ears, and the beets were stunted tiny things hardly the size of radishes. But these failures only led us to believe we had learned some lessons about what to plant. Things which hadn't done well were dropped from the next year's garden.

The second year when we went to rototill we were confronted with a dense crop of cedar seedlings beneath the big overhanging tree. Packed in at twenty five or thirty plants to the square foot, they had obviously found the tilled soil agreeable. Considerable hand weeding was needed before we could rototill again.

Over the years subsequent gardens have continued to produce semi-stunted vegetables and rusty water still gives that red film to foliage that never looks lushly green. The size of the plot has gradually been scaled down from that ambitious twelve foot by thirty five foot start. An orange plastic mesh now drapes over the wire of the original fence after we had trouble keeping out the neighbor's pet rabbits. An unnatural orange glow hits the eyes as you drive up the hill to the house. Oh, well, I tell myself, it matches the orange water.

Last year we built a couple small raised beds and did away with the whole idea of rototilling. We plant in almost pure compost. After all, the compost heap always grows the best plants. Even in that rich soil some refinements will be needed in the new beds, we are still learning.

Will we continue to do all this for our somewhat meager returns? Absolutely. I realize I like the process. Getting out in the warm spring weather to begin the planting and digging in the soil with bare hands is not a thing to be given up easily. And the taste of just a few fresh green beans and a couple of vine ripened tomatoes will keep me at it for many years. Always of course hoping for the miracle of bounty and lushness.

Learning the Flora

We used to spend the summers working not far from where we now live. We would arrive from the city in mid June, when school was out, and stay until the end of August. During those summers I became quite familiar with the flowers that bloomed in these mountains during the summer months. I looked forward to arriving when the ceanothus or wild lilac was in full flower, long after it had bloomed along the coast. In certain spots along the creeks one could first smell and then find wild azaleas. If you brought a branch home to brighten the cabin, the heady scent would almost overwhelm the small space.

On the drier east slope of the mountains where we spent those summers the wildflowers were always sparsely distributed. Each patch you came upon seemed a real treasure, a feast for the eyes. We watched for the yellow blazing star to appear along the roads. The bright flash of purple penstemon might reward you from roadside or forest glade. Even the subtle pale pink of dog bane and pussy paws were a pleasure to see. In the damper days of early summer there would be showy white lilies scattered among the trees. Their vibrant orange cousins the leopard lilies grew along the irrigation ditches and creek banks.

As the summer heated up and the land dried out, small yellow composites, the sort impossible to identify, and the single yellow flower of the mules ear surrounded by a corona of gray green leaves were the signs of late summer. The hardy penstemon seemed to last into early fall, its purple blooms contrasting with the dominant yellow blooms of August.

Living on the lusher western slope of the same mountains, and living there year round, we've had a whole new set of wildflowers to identify and enjoy as they emerge in the spring through summer cycle. In early spring we watch for tiny Johnny-jump-ups, looking like miniature yellow and maroon pansies. About the same time we search a marshy area on our property for the magenta colored flowers of the shooting stars. All their leaves flat to the earth, the flowers emerge at the end of long thin stalks, nodding slightly with the weight of the tiny blossoms.

71

Calicortis, palest lavender and softly fuzzy, and the wildly patterned orange and maroon fritilaria join the early spring blossoms.

As spring progresses we see the same lilies that grow on the east side, the white scented Washingtonia and the creekside complement of leopard lilies. And most pleasing to my eyes, greening up our pine needle covered ground, a small low trifoliate plant with the tiniest of pale pink flowers which we have identified as the Arctic star flower. It forms a sort of ground cover for a couple of months, drying out only as July heats up and the occasional rain is long past.

Our roadsides also bloom lushly with penstemon, a bluer variety than the purple ones of the east side. They mix with masses of Shasta daisies and lupines. Along one straight section of road the daisies and penstemon, backed by a wall of blue ceanothus against the green of the firs and pines, stretch for several miles. Altogether a lusher scene than across the range to the east.

Being here in spring, we also see the glorious redbud emerging and blossoming to a lavender pink froth. It is one of our first signs of fading winter. It appears a bit later on the cooler east side, something we never saw when we arrived in June. We knew it was there, but the flowering state makes the real visual impact, making you more aware of the presence of the plant. Another plant we knew was there but have come to notice and enjoy in its flowering state is the western dogwood. It also gives a show of turning red foliage in the fall.

Learning the native wildflowers and when and where to find them has been one of the chief rewards of living in the foothills. And when even our elevation has succumbed to sere dried out summer, we can drive a few miles up into the mountains and find an earlier season playing itself out in the high mountain meadows. There is much to be said for microclimates. They satisfy a need to see new fresh swaths of emerging wildflowers. The hiking is great exercise too.

Logging

Our new neighbor is logging his three acres today. Somehow I feel violated in the way you do when your car or house is broken into. Some of our privacy is disappearing and a lot of our sense if seclusion will be gone.

The neighbor's land lies between us and the nearest side road. Now I can see, not to mention hear, cars going by every few minutes. I knew the road was close but the dense thicket of trees kept the illusion of seclusion almost a reality. And the thick foliage reduced the traffic noise considerably.

The resident forester spoke frequently of the fact that the neighbor's trees were too thick, a dense fuel ladder ready to make short work of his tall trees as well as ours in a fire. We do worry about fire in our rainless California summers. Quite a few fires have come near enough in our six years residence to cause a persistent anxiety. That anxiety has led us to make an evacuation list which is tacked to the wall by the back door. We have become very conscious of forest fires.

So for fire safety reasons we are realistically accepting of some logging. But were the land ours, our approach would have been different. As we practice forestry on our land, the fuel ladder and smaller understory trees with little chance of breaking through the canopy of tall trees are the ones to be cut. We take this approach for both fire safety and to provide an ongoing source of fuel for our wood stove. We prize the fine old pines and cedars and the few massive black oaks in their midst. For noise and visual privacy we've left screens of smaller trees in certain areas. On our new neighbor's land everything over fourteen inches DBH (diameter breast height, a forestry term) is gone, along with much of the smaller foliage that could have screened us, and him, from roads and each other.

I am not able to watch as the trees come down. Taking a last look at the old giants to keep the sight in my memory, I retreat indoors as the saw whines and crashes occur. At day's end I patrol the bushwhacked property line hacked out by the surveyor before all this began. I marvel that even trees just his side of the line have been cut. I begin to see his reason, it can only be money. The aesthetics of nature do not enter the picture. That perhaps also settles the question of why he chose the site, where most who come and build value being in the tall forest. Was the choice for him simply a question of the immediate possibility of a monetary return to defray the cost of the land?

We wait in fear to see what measures will be taken with the willow lined swampy wetland that the creek flows into before crossing under the highway to a forested area. We imagine an attempt to prettify the banks and reduce reed grown mud-flats. The thick willows are now naturally reducing the amount of standing water but will he understand that? In my initial meeting with him I expressed the hope that the creek would be untouched. I was assured of that but was also led to believe, pre-logging, that screens and some tall trees would be left. That hasn't happened.

Perhaps in the spring leafed-out alders, young oaks and willows will screen us more than looks possible in the present winter landscape. But it will be noisier, the tall trees are gone, and gardening in the buff will no longer be a cherished pastime of the resident forester.

Small Has its Rewards

There are some definite rewards to living in a small community. Perhaps the best one is that the ratio of the people you know to the total population is much higher. You see someone you know every day if you are out and about. You needn't go to some special place, just the grocery store, the bank or the copy place will do.

People seem friendlier than in a large metropolitan area. Perhaps that's because you're going to run into someone you know more often, it's hard to hide in a small community. It's not easy to melt into the crowd when there really isn't one.

The friendliness even extends to times when you don't happen to run into your acquaintances. They contact you if they have something they want you to know about or if they think you'll be interested in a particular bit of information. There seems to be more of a sense of "I'm thinking about you and I'm not too busy with my hectic life to do something about it". How many times have I heard "I meant to call you but I just got so busy" in my urban life? More than I wish to recall. And I have not been free of the habit myself.

For years I have been exhibiting my artwork in group shows and a few one person shows. Most of these occurred in the large urban area where I lived for most of my adult life. Recently I had my first one person show in the small city which is the center of the rural area where I now live. I expected the usual response from friends and acquaintances. Their presence at a given show was always previously occasioned by an invitation to the opening. And if they came they were support-ive, even complementary, and I was appreciative. I never heard from anyone who didn't make it to the opening. The assumption was they were simply too busy to attend. I thought this was the norm.

I was more than a little surprised by the response to my show in the new location. I can't say who came to the opening, I didn't make it myself. The two week win-ter flu/cold/crud, or all of the above, had me at home curled up in a chair with a good book and a cup of tea just waiting to feel better. Going by past knowledge of how openings go, I thought I would never know whether anyone had been there.

Within days of the opening of the show I got the first congratulatory phone call from a friend. She hadn't gone to the opening event either, but made a point of attending on her own time. A few days later I got the first card from another acquaintance who had seen the show. Within days there were more phone calls, another card. When I was out and about again I began running into friends and acquaintances who all wanted to let me know they had enjoyed the show and tell me what they liked best. Weeks after the show had closed I was still running into people who had laudatory comments. I was a bit overwhelmed by the reactions. I eventually concluded it was as satisfying as getting a good critical review. And much more gratifying to be told in person.

Would it have happened in the city? I think not. Size, hurry, sheer numbers of people, all combine to make the chance of seeing someone you know slim or next to improbable in the course of an ordinary day. Maybe city dwellers just know more people and therefore need to divide their time available to associate with each friend into smaller pieces. If that is true, the friendliness of small communities is a definite reward for living in a rural area.

Back Roads Neighbors

Exploring back roads on our mountain ridge we found a spot where a creek cuts a gorge through the soft rock backbone of the land. Layer upon layer of the sedimentary base of the ridge stands exposed in the deep chasm formed by the tumbling waters. Today the creek was at flood stage, pouring tea colored water through the narrow defile. The deep stream-carved canyon is a gashed surprise in the otherwise level ridge top.

We came on a couple of unexpected places in that backwoods region, one on either side of the deep canyon. One was a disheveled house and its numerous outbuildings in a muddy clearing littered with old cars and cast off machinery. A troop of motley dogs patrolled the fenced perimeter, looking more surprised at the intrusion of outsiders than intent on guarding the property. A man watched curiously from a rundown porch but gave no response to our wave.

Walking down a dirt road which edged the canyon of the roaring creek we came upon a cabin built on stilts at the end of the road where the ridge falls away in moss covered rocks to the creek eighty feet below. A room wide cabin hunkered into the hillside. The airborne deck surrounding the cabin had a view upstream of a twisted notch now booming in a thirty foot waterfall the color of green tea. Fully shuttered and amply locked, the place had the appearance of a summer retreat. "Whispering Waters" proclaimed a large wood sign suspended overhead between two tall trees. The creek must run softly in the summer. Perhaps the owners had not experienced the booming waters of a near flood such as now urgently pushed its way through the resisting rock ledges.

As if to confirm our thoughts, a dim fading penciled sign was tacked to the near corner of the cabin. It listed the contents of the cabin, then proclaimed, "If you must break in anyway, please clean up after yourself. We come here for the sake of memory, not for a working vacation." As an afterthought, further deterrent, or thoughtful bit of information, a last line stated "And the water has worms in it, I advise you not to drink it." There were no signs of forced entry. The worms must be a positive deterrent.

I am intrigued by the contrast between these two backwoods neighbors, their houses not more than a half mile apart on opposite banks of the stream. The occupants of the cluster of old buildings in the muddy clearing appear to be living a subsistence existence, hanging on to every scrap as possibly useful in the future, unable to throw anything away. Hand to mouth looks to be the rule of their day.

The builder of the cabin has to have a romantic soul. There is a shelf of flat land where his room wide cabin would have fit. But he built it clinging to the land in back, and flying over the precipice in front. The memories for which he returns could not be as poignant without that air beneath the wings of his deck.

Fences

There are few fences in our rural forested part of the state. The ones we do have are the barbed wire variety, designed to keep cattle and livestock confined to a certain area. Wooden fences of the type common in the city, defining one's small urban territory from the neighbor's, are scarcely needed in an area where acre plus lots are the norm.

When we moved to our three acre forest land we felt almost isolated. There was only one other house we could see from ours. We were screened from nearby roads by our trees and those of our neighbors whose plots were of similar size. Though we backed up on a subdivision, those lots too maintained the mixed forest cover unique to the area. We felt we were deeper in the country than we really were. The urban feeling of needing to be constantly on guard for one's property and person seemed unnecessary in our new rural environment.

Chance visitors were rare, anyone who came by was someone we expected. We locked our doors at night and when we were away but felt quite safe leaving things open when we were around. The garage and barn remained unlocked and often open. Boats, ladders, and garden tools were more or less stored outside where they were used. The only fence on our property was around an old pig run adjoining the barn.

Our neighbor does have a fence, a cyclone fence six feet in height surrounding his three acres. It is the only urban type structure in our area. He did not install the fence, it was there when he bought the place. It was apparently originally put up to protect and enclose a herd of fallow deer kept by a previous owner. That original purpose for the fence I could accept as fitting for a rural lifestyle. The way our current neighbor regards the fence has much more of an embattled urban attitude to it. His attitudes have changed the way I look at the fence.

For the first few years I almost managed to not see the fence. Aesthetically it always offended me. I trained my eyes to focus on the forest beyond the fence, to let the metal chain links fade into a half focus. If I thought about it, I tried remembering that once a graceful herd of deer grazed beyond its cold metal regularity. It seemed adequate reason for its otherwise urban intrusion on the rural scene. As we have come to know our neighbor, I have become convinced that the fence was part of the appeal of the property when he decided to purchase it. His move from a heavily urbanized part of the state seemed to have quite a bit of the survivalist mentality attached to his desire to settle in a rural area.

Behind the fence he and his family established a mini-farm. They soon had several goats, rabbits in legions, chickens, ducks and a ferocious set of patrol dogs who continue after five years of neighborship to bark in outrage at our every move. Well confined as they are, though the rabbits do manage to visit our attempts at a flower garden, we have had no problem accepting the proximity of the animals. As we've watched the compaction of the earth and the contrived gravelization of the stream bank of the creek we share, we have however come to view the enterprise as an urban dream transplanted to the country. As if their idea of a farm has been untouched by the forest environment in which they now find themselves. We've taken to calling it the 'LA Urban Dream Farm'.

The cyclone fence meanwhile, seems more and more appropriate for what lies within its three acre perimeter. Its locked gate with buzzer gives off the feeling of a bastion mentality as much as the barking dogs who patrol its edges. I find myself noticing the fence more often, it is hard to make it fade into soft focus anymore.

In spite of our slightly offended aesthetic and environmental senses, we have a good relationship with the neighbors. Good but at the same time distant, the fence is constantly between us. Early in our relationship they expressed the desire to be left alone. As we felt somewhat the same way that was fine with us. We each had our reasons for moving to a place in the country. And yet we watch out for each other's property, letting each other know if we'll be away for a while or if something seems out of the ordinary.

A recent incident brought home again how we each feel so differently about our rural surroundings. On a dark stormy evening our neighbor knocked on our front door. He couldn't find our phone number so had driven over. We rarely use our front door and seldom leave outside lights on. He'd had to stumble in from the driveway to find our door. He was packing a small pistol. Our mutual back neighbor had called, he told us, to say he'd seen three young men carrying something jump over our neighbor's cyclone fence. The ever alert patrol dogs had frightened them off but they might be on our land and might take something. We said we had little of value outside to be stolen.

"Do you have a gun?" he asked.

"An old shotgun," my husband replied, not adding that he didn't know where the shells were and hadn't had it out in years.

"Better get it out" said our neighbor. "At least I have my fence, it's security. You don't have that." And don't feel anywhere near as embattled or threatened, we thought to ourselves.

We determined the next day that nothing had been taken from his place or ours. Probably kids on a lark we decided. But a few days later while standing at our kitchen window my eye caught a flash of color which was out of place with the normally tree filled view beyond the cyclone fence. Our neighbor had felt compelled to post a 'No Trespassing' sign on a tree. It is a pulsing day-glow orange and is oriented on an angle facing both our property and the rear fence from whence the intruders came. We know it is for potential trespassers but its orientation toward us is just a trifle disconcerting. Since we won't provide a buffer fence we must suffer the tangible view of his fortress mentality. And it makes soft focusing through the fence even more difficult, the day-glow orange sign ruins the effect.

For our part we still feel fine without a fence. Maybe the lack of one even adds to an impression there is nothing of value to steal here. Just our trees and woods, reminding us we are far from urban pressures.

Lists and Accomplishments

I accomplished eleven things today. I made a list in the morning and dutifully, happily, with a deep sense of achievement, crossed each item off as I completed it. But wait, how about the extra things I did? The things I thought of as I was in the middle of another task. Shouldn't I add them to the list, make it reflect the fourteen things I actually did? And what about the making of the list itself, doesn't that count?

The list assures me that I've had a most successful day, even when the items include the likes of things such as laundry, vacuum and change linens. Everything counts on my list. But what have I really done? The list also includes items such as, take time to write, set up the loom for weaving two rugs, design a rug to be woven after the current two are finished. When several of these meaty items are on the same list, there are usually one or two that don't get crossed off by day's end.

But a list always satisfies me most when it has a number of items on it. The sheer numbers fit with my increasingly shortened attention span. I seem to be able to stick with an activity only briefly, maybe an hour or two, in contrast to my previous ability to pursue one activity all day. Maybe it's the fact that I work at home now. My studio is just another room in the house, not a real getaway place. I can never leave the needs of housework behind and immerse myself totally in the artwork. The dirty kitchen floor screams at me as I walk through, the smudged windows in the studio cry out for a cleaning.

As I take a break to tend to these mundane chores, several things seem to compensate for tearing myself away from creativity. I'm putting my break time to good use. I usually continue thinking about the creative activity at hand as I go about the chores. In fact, some of the best designing takes place as I mop the floor or put together a casserole for dinner. And I can cross another item of the list! Of course I may need to add it to the list first. That's even better, there will be a fifteenth item to add to my day's accomplishments.

This is the organized part of my brain taking over. Sometimes I hate it. I just want to have a day with nothing planned, no lists. I want to drift into one or another creative activity unfettered by the need to get it done by a particular time. Sometimes I do that. But then the day comes when the list making instinct creeps back.

I designed a great rug yesterday, I can't wait to start on it. Today I'll plan the materials I need for it, order the yarns, finish the scarves on the loom to free it for the rug. That's three things to do, the start of a great list. And if I include the newly chopped wood I stacked, the mending, the blackberries I picked for the freezer, that makes six things on the list.

New Technologies

Our children long ago decided their parents were either technological idiots or decidedly far behind the times when it came to acquiring new technologies. For ten or twelve years I used an old treadle foot sewing machine my mother-in-law had long relegated to her basement. We were married six years before we had a television. It was given to us by a friend who felt sorry for our deprived state. He didn't realize it was as much choice as lack of disposable income which kept us from getting a TV. The old black and white model he gave us was not replaced by a color TV for another nine years.

A primitive record player didn't give way to a stereo system until the kids were in their teens. They had lost all hope at that point and were surprised and amazed by our purchase. They of course knew immediately how to use it. They were in college before we felt ready to tackle a VCR. On that occasion they merely shrugged at our incompetence with advanced technology and proceeded to teach us how to use it.

Our oldest son gave us our first microwave oven. To my surprise it revolutionized my cooking patterns. At first I used it mostly to defrost frozen foods but what a change in my daily routine it brought about. I didn't have to even think about dinner until time to cook it. I still don't use it much for actual cooking but I wouldn't want to live without it.

Moving from a cosmopolitan, urban life to a home in a rural area definitely didn't mean I was a technological savant giving up a host of modern conveniences. Indeed the pattern of taking years to adjust to the mere idea of a new convenience, not to mention actually acquiring something everyone else had long accepted as commonplace, was actually disrupted when we bought the house in the country. It had a dishwasher. We'd never considered getting one for the small kitchen in our old city house. What would the kids do for chores if there weren't dishes to wash? When it was my turn to wash the dishes I convinced myself I rather enjoyed the quiet uninterrupted moments of routine work. But now the kids were grown and the chores had devolved on us, maybe we could learn to use that dishwasher.

In other aspects the new house did take us backwards along the technological path. A wood stove was the primary heat source. This form of heat proved to require significant amounts of exercise and personal heat expenditure before the house itself showed any warming effects. Constant attention was also a prerequisite for maintaining a comfortable climate. We soon longed for the ease of our old forced air furnace. The trade between time spent washing dishes and that required to keep the house warm was decidedly uneven.

One night when there were a particularly large number of dirty dishes and the wood stove had seemed to occupy the greater part of my day I decided it was time to learn to use the dishwasher. It was an old machine with no instructions, appropriate perhaps for us technological dinosaurs. I knew that dishwashers used special soap but I hadn't bought any. I had the vague notion that it was all a way of getting people to buy yet another product anyway. Soap is soap, right? I'd just use the regular dishwashing soap I always had on hand. Into the little box on the door of the dishwasher it went. I closed the door quickly as the liquid soap began to ooze out of the box and run down the door. I pushed what looked like the appropriate buttons. Whirring noises emitted from the machine and I left the room satisfied that I had conquered yet another new technology.

Ten minutes later I went back into the kitchen for something. I was greeted by the sight of a few small mounds of soap suds on the floor beneath the dishwasher. As I gazed in fascination more and more mounds of frothy bubbles emerged from the sides of the door. I called for help and quickly we were vainly scooping up heaps of suds and dumping then in the sink. Soon we were laughing so hard that keeping ahead of the process was impossible. The sink was heaped high with bubbles which wouldn't go down the drain and even on the rinse cycle more suds kept emerging from the machine. A complete second cycle, without any soap at all, was required to flush out the machine and make the dishes useable.

With our technological idiocy fully in evidence, we might have been discouraged about using the dishwasher. We did however go on to understand and use the new machine. Having mastered that device we were emboldened to wonder what we might try next. Satellite TV? Being thirty miles from the nearest city and limited in reception to two channels, we gave that idea serious consideration. But considering that we never watched the commercial channel we could get, being too annoyed with the predominance of the advertising, we decided the last thing we needed was a plethora of commercial channels which we would choose not to watch. We had a good educational channel available and decided we could survive on that and have some time left for reading and listening to music. We did purchase a CD player, returning it only once for more explicit instructions on its use. The kids weren't there to help us learn to use it.

We haven't decided on our next technological advance, but no doubt it will be something everyone else has been using for ten years by the time we have the courage to join them.

Repeat Performance

It's not often one gets the chance to relive a section of one's earlier life. I was granted that opportunity when I decided to do some graduate work at the decidedly uncollegiate time of middle age. Being back on campus after a gap of almost thirty years proved to be a great experience, if not exactly an actual repeat of the undergraduate years.

I was sure I'd be the only gray haired middle aged woman in evidence, more like a visiting parent than a fellow student to the throngs of kids who were even younger than my own children. So it was with some trepidation similar to the early days of a freshman's introduction to college that I approached the first few days. To my vast relief there were several obviously older women in my classes as well as a few men out of their twenties. No one was asking ages but we all felt some comfort in each others company. And the 'kids', as we referred to anyone under twenty two, were accepting and even expressed admiration for our presence, recognizing that we were validating the worth of advanced education by our return to school at an older age.

Though acceptance as fellow students came unexpectedly easily, it seemed more difficult for some of the professors to accept our presence. Many of us were the same age or older than our teachers and one or two seemed uncertain how to treat us. But most accepted our being there as a mark of our desire to partake of their knowledge. Over time both they and we older students appreciated the different sort of interaction possible by our approaching the subject at hand with some life experience, something not yet within the capability of the younger students. The insights of we older students sparked added life into many a class discussion.

Friendships developed in unexpected places, not just with people of the same age. There was Josie, the young Chinese wife of a high school teacher. Bright and eager to learn about her adopted country, she was a bubbly addition to any class. Leslie was in her early thirties, a single mother struggling to make a better life for herself and two young children by taking advanced work. It was never easy for her and we all did what we could to help. Bill was about thirty five, a jack-of-all trades trying to earn a degree which would make use of his multiple talents. Cat was my age, the divorced mother of three grown children, resolved to advance her possibilities in life and provide an example to her kids. Antoinette was in her mid twenties, a native of a Caribbean island. Culturally she was vastly out of place and hugely homesick, but determined to get a Masters degree to take home to her island. I became both her friend and surrogate mother, an interpreter of northern California culture and a provider of an occasional care package of her beloved rice and beans when her meager funds ran low.

And then there was my own son, a recent college graduate who decided to enter the same graduate program. During the year we were in school together we became not just parent and child but adult friends, an experience both of us greatly value. I was a bit ahead of him in the program but we did have one class together. Both the professor and the other students regarded us with a bemused interest which we each rather enjoyed. It was a class in Native American Art, a topic of great interest to both of us. We completed the class with the two highest grades, a mother-son feat which was a first for the university.

My greatest reward from that three years of graduate work was the intense pleasure of using my mind. Unlike my undergraduate years, which were intense in a quite different fashion, I was able to regard the work as enjoyable for its own sake. What I have taken from that time is a continued interest in educating myself, in the ongoing pursuit of knowledge. I only wish I could have cultured that attitude as an undergraduate, how much more I would have gotten from that period in my life.

Edges

Sometimes it rains on one side of my house but not the other. This phenomenon always gives me a feeling of excitement, of having discovered a great truth. What I've discovered is an edge, and that even the weather has edges.

Edges are places or moments or events whose main characteristic is one of contrast. Things or words or ideas are juxtaposed which are inherently opposite or different. In humor, irony and paradox both deal with contrast. Nature is full of edges, the meeting points of contrasting ecosystems. Meadow and forest, stream and bank, lake and shore, ocean and land, cloud and sunlight all meet at an edge.

If you live near an ocean, the concept of an edge is something you understand intuitively. Hard to define, the presence of the sea matters to your well being. It does not matter if you visit it often, its atmosphere is part of your sense of place, just knowing it is there is important.

Now residing about two hundred miles inland, I commented recently to a friend from the Midwest that I miss the ocean. With great seriousness, she asked me "how do you use the ocean?" As if my answer would explain my missing it. Momentarily speechless, my mind's eye saw myself in a small boat venturing out on the Pacific's great swells, felt the cold chill of feet gingerly placed in the surf, the tug of a rock cod on the end of a line, watched a fog bank approaching the shore.

While these have all been part of my experience, these things are not the reason I miss the ocean. How to explain my longing for the mere presence of the ocean, the salt in the air, the ever changing light and weather at its rim? All I could think of to explain it was the concept of an edge. It offers a change, a contrast. Something else is on the other side, another edge, a new experience. Each new encounter with that edge is a discovery, a new finding of that great fascination with the meetings of contrasts. It defines my place on one edge and presents another to be explored by the mind and the senses. How else to explain the desire and ability to sit hours at a time on the shore watching wave patterns. And to rise and in turn be fascinated by the plants and creatures which inhabit the edge of the land. It's all about edges.

Volunteering

Riding along a gravel road on the crest of the north Warner Mountains, I try to concentrate on the mission at hand. I have accompanied my scientist husband as a volunteer on a trip in search of a particular insect. Finding a tiny insect in a forest is similar to, well, that needle in the haystack business.

We are trying to spot the creature by looking for ravages to the new growth on white fir trees. Learning just what to look for is not easy, a light browning at the tips of this year's growth along with signs of the foliage having been chewed. My major problem is the distraction of riding up a high mountain road on a summer morning as the sun is just warming up the meadows and woods.

A cool breeze wafts in the open truck windows. It carries faint hints of redolent fir needles, pungent sage and the slightly musty smell of the bright yellow wyethia flowers carpeting the high meadows. The sun is just at tree top level, leaving the ground in cool shadow. I should be watching each passing fir tree for signs of the elusive diorhichtria but my eye is too often caught by tiny flashes of color among the green foliage of emerging wildflowers. I want to see and identify every one, ever watchful for something not seen before.

The scientist is able to navigate the washboard surface of the road and still scan the ranked foliage of each passing fir. And I'm constantly distracted by the flowers. Determined, I drag my attention back to the firs and the insect we're seeking.

We must look closely as this particular insect shares a niche with several closely related creatures. Browning behind the new growth, on last year's needles, could be sawflies or needleminers. The succulent bright green growth of the current year may be shared with the Modoc budworm. Finding singed looking branches is first, than a closer examination is needed to find the correct creatures.

The firs look vibrantly healthy this year. Some years there are major outbreaks of the insects which devastate the foliage, especially if several of the bug populations explode in the same season. I finally spot some singed foliage on my side of the truck. I remark on it but decide it is probably damage from last year. Patiently, and on the off chance I may have found something, the scientist stops the truck and we get out to examine the tree. "You were right, it is feeding from last year, but now you know what you're looking for." Heartened by my educational advancement, I search with new intensity. Until the breeze and the flowers call again.

By early afternoon we are still searching. It is definitely not a year to worry about an outbreak. The magic of early morning has worn off. I am glad the fir forest is at high elevation. Seen off the crest, the valley below is beginning to shimmer with heat.

Then on a narrow dirt road the branches of a thick patch of young firs all but thrust their foliage in the open truck windows. The new needles are singed and distorted from recent chewing. On closer examination we find groups of sawfly larvae feeding just behind the new growth. And out on the growing tips are little tent wrapped bundles of needles with tiny white larvae feeding inside. Could it be the diorhichtria? The scientist is not sure at this point that we have found the exact insect we are looking for. We will need to take some back to the lab for rearing to determine if the search was successful.

We both begin finding more of the small tents and I am able to contribute more to my volunteering venture than simply holding the open plastic bag to receive the captured specimens. Thus mollified, I can return to enjoyment of the sun and the setting and the wildflowers. How nice that the insect we sought inhabits such a place. I'll be happy to volunteer to search for it again.

High Country Spring

Words do poor justice to the feel of a spring day in the high country.

Smells, sounds, the very feel of the air serve as description.

Sky, air, earth, are all so cleanly pure,

having emerged from the snow wraps of six months winter isolation.

The eye sees a limited palette,

straw colored ground,

brown and green of standing pines,

the aching blue of sky over all.

The crowns of trees sway in a wind more heard than seen.

At ground level little moves,

but circling the ridge is a rushing sound, keeping its distance.

The sky is a clear blue arcing over the ridge,

an unbroken surround of inverted bowl.

The bright sun would be hot at lower elevations,

at six thousand feet it is cooled by altitude and the high breeze above.

The spring sun is heating up the forest floor,

warming slowly to summer's baking dryness.

Pine needles and bunch grass give off a toasted redolence,

recycling to become this year's addition to the humus underfoot.

In some low spots, winter snow melt stands blackly waiting to evaporate.

The first green grasses sprout through its inches of dark depth,

promise of a few weeks of summer lushness.

Above lingering snow banks, small intact worlds of winter,

the air is twenty degrees cooler than the surrounding atmosphere.

As the day warms, the wind shifts down in closer circles,

wafting scents of resin, sage, and

faint hints of vanilla from the pine trunks.

An early bumble bee buzzes faintly,

searching fruitlessly for early blooms.

A few butterflies float on random zephyrs,

performing their own private dance to spring.

A crush of needles underfoot, a pinch of sage in the fingers,

a sniff of rifted pine bark, the feel of a warm rock under the hand,

these enhance the feel of the day, and must serve for future memories.

The Devil's Garden

The red hued ribbon of the dirt road is a fine contrast to the new green grass and
pine needles.

Old ponderosa trunks accent the green with upward slashes of rusty red color.

The dusky blue gray sage returns the eye to the arc of blue overhead.

Low growing wildflowers greet the observant viewer, tiny flashes of intense
blue and yellow.

Perhaps because summer dryness has largely kept humans away,
the place supports abundant wildlife.

Antelope are often visible on sagebrush flats, deer keep their distance,
being prized by humans and therefore wary.

Golden eagles boldly survey their personal domains from snag or fence post,
unafraid and dominant.

Sand hill cranes move about in close pairs, regal in their size and stately flight.

They call it the Devil's Garden, no doubt for its limited seasonal water and
abundance of lava rock.

But on a spring day in May it has a charm, a sparse lushness in small meadows
and creeks flowing thinly over rocky ledges.

One could do worse than share this Devil's landscape on a warm day in late spring.

Devil's Garden Reprise

Spring's crisp colors are muting to a summer dryness,

the high contrast of spring hues now replaced by a softened palette.

The sharp green of early grass and vivid intensity of spring's first flowers

have lost their brightness.

Summer's flowers are lighter hued, paler,

blending to the dominant silvery blue-gray sage.

Softly blue wild flax blossoms, dusty green upthrust leaves of mules ears

merge colors with omnipresent sage.

The red road is baking to the sere dryness of a terra cotta pot.

Reddish pine trunks now are dusted to a grayed brown,

lacking the moisture sheen of springtime,

they no longer read as rusty slashes pointing skyward.

Even the aching blue spring sky is muted by the land's reflectant warmth,

softened by afternoon cloud puffs to a powdery blue.

Black rocks which glistened under spring runoff reveal

now a dusty cover of the last freshet's silty flow.

Shrunken pools sit blackly waiting for summer heat

to rob the land of all moisture.

Once lush meadows are sered to crisp yellow at their drying fringes.

Summer's hot hand is gripping tighter,

when water will be but a memory on the land,

an unfulfilled promise in the sky.

Transplanted Wilderness

Living with a field biologist, I've gotten to experience a lot of half wild places as his official and most frequent volunteer. His research requires field experiments in a lot of spots most people never get to, though many aren't far off main roads. Logging roads are his main avenue to the plots he sets up to study tree growth and response to natural enemies.

One of his more ambitious recent studies has been the ongoing research into the natural history of a brush patch of very dense manzanita. Manzanita grows up quickly after a fire or a clearcutting. It crowds out young pines or firs, producing, in the forester's view, an undesirable cover. Manzanita seems to have few natural enemies or diseases. Once established, nothing seems to bother it.

One of the reasons I enjoy being the number one volunteer is the aesthetic setting of many of the experiments in beautiful forested areas. I can't say the manzanita patch fell into this category. It was hot and dusty, a dry site on a rocky slope. The sameness of the vegetation quickly grew visually boring. There were only a few hardy firs poking up through the eight foot tall manzanita cover to provide some visual relief.

The ambitious project involved the building of an eight foot tall fence around two acres of manzanita brush. A cover of bird netting was sewn together in long strips to make a continuous top which rested on the fence. This kept out birds and allowed the study of the hoped for ravages of insects saved from avian beaks. The scientific term for the hoped for results is biological control.

Pressed into service the first autumn along with the graduate students involved in the research, I had helped to roll the huge net for winter storage. Over the winter it disintegrated in spots. Its replacement was made of the bright orange plastic mesh you see along highway construction sites. It was heavier, stiffer, generally unwieldy, and I bowed out of volunteering where that plot was concerned. The new plastic net cover even proved a bit much for the fence which held it up. It was decided to contract out to have a stronger fence built. And to have the same crew roll out the new cover.

The biologist found he could hire a crew from one of the minimum security prison camps which are scattered around our rural part of the state. Under the direction of a Forest Service Supervisor they are often seen clearing and thinning trees and brush along the edges of state highways. Clad in jeans, hard hats and boots and looking every inch rural, these men are often city boys getting their first taste of the country.

At the manzanita plot, on a logging road about a mile off a main highway but rarely visited except by a few locals, the crew quite soon felt they were in a wilderness. Arriving one morning to check their progress, the biologist and I found them gaping over bear tracks visible in the dust of the logging road. "Man, this must be wild country." they said. "Not sure I want to be up there in that brush. Maybe we need a lookout." Reassured by their supervisor, they proceeded to work. But not without frequent wary looks over their shoulders.

They drove the eighty miles from their camp each morning in a bus. They brought their lunch and the makings for snacks and coffee at break time. This was all highly preferable to sitting around the barracks in the camp. They were happy each day they got to go somewhere to work, wilderness or not. Arrived at the work site, it was one man's duty to remain at the bus, build a campfire, brew pots of coffee and get the meal ready. It was a duty assigned after one had put in long months on the physical labor end of the operation. It was a task reserved for those nearing release.

Diego was a city boy from San Jose. At home he was street wise from an early age, though it hadn't saved him from the trouble that landed him in jail. He was looking forward to his release in a few months. It hadn't been easy for any of his relatives to travel the three hundred miles to visit him during the time he'd been at the camp. He'd recently graduated to campfire duty and was proud of keeping the fire going and the coffee pot boiling on its stick propped over the fire. Just like in the old West he said.

He told us he'd jump in the bus or get near the fire if the bear came around again. His job was easier than doing the hard stuff the boys were doing up the hill. It was pretty easy duty he guessed. But lately he'd seen some real scary things along the road, not just the bear tracks. There were all these pickups going by, (it was fall and the hunting season had begun) they must be hunters. "But man, it was creepy, they had all these guns, man, on racks in their cabs." And they looked like bad dudes, there was no way he wanted to tangle with them.

No doubt, on his turf, the hunters would have felt the same about Diego. Wilderness is where you find it.

Symbols

At a long treasured spot in the mountains we discovered a wildflower new to us. It was always there, probably we just arrived slightly earlier in the season than on previous visits. But this newly discovered flower seemed to symbolize the place in a way no previous discoveries had ever done. Columbia windflower, a wild anemone, even its name captures the spirit of the high mountain ridge, narrowly dividing watersheds, a foothold for breathtaking views of ranges rolling endlessly away both north and south. Each bloom's glossy white bowl of petals flutters in the breezes meandering at the base of the great red firs where the flowers are often found.

We have long loved the area, returning year after year to savor the ridge top views and cool breezes, the open grassy glades and drifts of wildflowers, the magnificent old red fir groves. To find a new flower in one of the places we loved the most, the camping spot we returned to so often, was an unexpected gift, a new memory to treasure. A reason to return and search it out again. A reminder that new things can be found in old beloved places.

The flower discovery came at dusk, as we hiked up the dusty road from the camping site to the crest of the ridge. As the light faded, it became too dim to search out any new botanical discoveries. Stretch the legs then, savor the breeze wafting down from the ridge crest, watch for deer browsing in the glade below.

As we climbed higher in the gathering dark, the view to the northwest opened wide below. Range after range of dusky ridges lay purpling in the distance. Each farther ridge muted its color, gradating to a dusky gray-blue in the far distance. At the horizon's edge the mountains met the soft orange haze left by the departed sun. The sky itself was not a simple wash of faded sunset color, but a slow suffusion from orange to lemon yellow.

To capture the scene was beyond the capacity of my point and shoot camera. I stood transfixed to imprint it in memory, willing it to recur in the mind's eye and perhaps in some future artwork. Along with the windflower, that late evening view will remain as symbol of a wild and beautiful place.

Strangers in the Night

The varied proclivities of our neighbors should not have surprised us, after all we were camped in an area specified as 'dispersed camping'. All that really meant was that there were no designated campsites, no tables, and most important to many of today's recreational vehicle campers, no level asphalt parking pads. As we came to realize however, it might also have meant that one could expect to find as fellow campers people dispersed or divergent in their lifestyles as well as their views of what camping is all about.

We try to camp with a minimum of equipment, though there are certain accoutrements which we feel we must have on every camping trip. There is our folding table with built in seats, our propane camp stove and battery powered lantern, a five gallon water container with a spigot at the base which gives a passable simulation of 'running' water, and a carefully chosen selection of old but serviceable cookware whose main characteristics have to be that they are easy to clean. The camp stove and lantern are new additions to the inventory, having replaced twenty five year old versions which ran on white gas. We feel we have moved up in the world, no more pumping and refilling with liquid white gas. But at the same time we wonder if we haven't gotten a touch too modern, somehow gone a bit too technological for the spirit of camping out. We think that way for about five minutes, until we realize the ease of using our new equipment is very pleasant. And after all, the white gas versions were already a big step away from the grill over the campfire and a candle stuck in a tin cup.

We have even dispensed with the campfires. Some people would say you aren't really camping without a fire in the evening. But on this occasion it was hot, and we are more conscious of the possibility of wildfires developing from improperly tended campfires, and most campgrounds don't allow the gathering of wood, and the kids are grown up and the demand for Smores is no longer a pressing issue requiring the nightly building of a fire. So we usually walk in the evening until nightfall, then read and write journals for an hour or so before turning in early.

So that pretty much describes our camping philosophy. We not only try not to make an impact that is obvious after we leave, we try not to make the impact too great while we are there. Just the essentials please. Spend the rest of the time enjoying the uniqueness of the place where you find yourself privileged to be for a few days.

Though we value our approach to camping, we hardly expect everyone else to have the same attitudes. So we were not surprised by the first group that moved in next to us in the 'dispersed' campground. Not surprised, but a bit amazed by the extent of the preparations needed to set up their camp. A man and two adolescent boys arrived in a pickup pulling a small trailer. For the next three hours we watched as a multitude of equipment and objects was taken from the two vehicles. It was a virtual camping equivalent of twenty clowns emerging from a tiny car at the circus.

First came a pop-up nylon tent and two cabin style canvas tents, each with a six by eight piece of plywood for flooring. They were arranged in a semi-circle with the trailer like pioneer wagons circled for the night. The central space was designated as a kitchen area with numerous coolers and cooking equipment. Over all was stretched a huge tarp. When the basic camp was in shape, out came the air mattresses, the bicycles, the inner tubes and the inflatable kayak. The pickup was started again and all the previous items were attached to the exhaust pipe via a hose and blown up for immediate use. We could not imagine how three people were going to need all that equipment. But not until the next evening did anyone else arrive. Then it seemed more plausible.

There were even some objects which apparently they had neglected to leave at home. The morning after their arrival we noticed two lipstick red plush lounge chairs out behind the trailer. They looked entirely out of place and apparently had been designated to the back of the camp where they would not be seen or used. It was actually difficult to imagine just where they would be at home. Were they fancy poolside loungers or exotic car seats? We could only stare at them in wonder.

Much of the first evening was taken up with chopping firewood. We could hear the sound of splitting logs far into the night. Every hour or so the pickup engine was started up to inflate some forgotten object or perhaps simply to play the radio. We found ourselves being surprised that they did not have a small generator with which to run everything. They seemed to have every other imaginable piece of modern camping equipment. But the lack of a generator did save on noise, the pickup truck engine was considerably quieter.

The second afternoon a group of four families arrived to occupy the campsite adjacent to that of our neighbors. With a large crew of men, women and children all helping, they soon had a tidy camp. As the women drifted by our campsite in their short sleeved summer dresses and little nets on the hair at the back of their heads, we surmised that they were a group of Mennonites. The men wore crisply ironed summer clothes and neatly trimmed beards. Their clothing seemed to indicate no recognition of the fact that dirt goes with the territory when one is camping.

Late that afternoon the Mennonites also set off in search of firewood, returning dragging several medium sized logs. Long into the evening they too were chopping wood, the sound of the ax bouncing off the dry wood with a hollow ring.

Meanwhile the activity in our immediate neighbor's camp centered around the teenage son's rap music and the sounds of a card game. Though not terribly loud, the music was insidious, sounds spread so easily in a campground. Every half hour or so the truck engine was started up to power some piece of equipment or inflate another air mattress.

As if in response to the rap music, there was a sudden burst of singing from the Mennonite camp, where a huge bonfire now crackled in the hot evening air. The women harmonized on a repertoire of hymns, while the men continued chopping wood. Next door the rap music went off but the card game continued, the loud shuffling of cards carrying over the sonorous music from the adjacent camp. Side by side the sounds of the sacred and the profane continued into the late evening. When all was finally dark and the campfires reduced to glowing embers, there was a last burst of ululating sound from the Mennonite tents. The sacred triumphant over the profane, having the final word of the day.

Five Senses on a Summer Afternoon

Sight: A triangle formed by two lines of nylon blue tent and the mossy trunk of a bay frames life-green interlaced with branches, chlorophyll working for the life of tree and air.

Sound: Breeze and birds, the insistent buzz of flies. A raucous jay announcing his presence now here, now there. The skitter of small birds in brambles and drying leaves, their secret purposes revealed only by the dry rasp of movement. The sough of the wind high in tall bays, the rattle of an occasional falling yellowed leaf, done with its life season. Low, low beneath, the river's smooth run and fractured small sounds as it riffles over stony shallows.

Smell: Ripe sun warmed blackberries. Pungent bay leaves.

Touch: Warm air when the breeze blows. Sweat which attracts insistent crawling flies.

Taste: Cool water to quench the heat. Ripe melting blackberries stolen at each pass of a nearby bramble patch.

Blackberry Picking

When the mornings are fall, the afternoons summer, the blackberries are ripe.

Hot midday sun, dry golden grasses smelling of fall,

the berries matured to clusters of tiny grape-like globes.

Juicy plump berries fall in the hand as you touch to pick them.

As many in the mouth as in the bowl until the face and hands are purple stained.

The bucket soon has a pool of purple-red juice as the harvest grows.

Plenty for dessert and some left for breakfast.

I remember now how the milk turns purple when you heap them over

a bowl of granola.

A lovely silky purplish-mauve, it's not a color you see anywhere else.

If I could have a dress just that color, I would always recall hot fall afternoons,

The taste of ripe berries and the purplish-mauve milk in the cereal bowl.

Second Guessing Nature, Lament for a Forest

Over a period of some twenty years I have been privileged to visit a very special fir forest in the mountains of northern California. Over fifty years ago it was set aside as an experimental forest because of its incredible capacity as a growing site for both white and red firs. Covering a low mountain top east of the main Sierra and Cascade ranges, it was designated and set aside for research before commercial logging had penetrated to its somewhat remote area. As roads and timber harvesting reached farther into the backcountry it remained an island of old growth in a sea of increasingly sparse second growth forests.

To visit the forest in the 1970s allowed one to imagine the country as it was for eons, sustained by the native peoples and regarded with wonder by the early European visitors. For the scientists who worked there it provided opportunity for the study of a natural ecosystem largely untouched by the hand of man.

The forest could tell us important things if we asked the right questions. For those privileged to visit as professionals or as their assistants (few visited for other reasons though the area was always open to the public) it also offered an aesthetic experience, if you were open to it.

The forest in the 1970s could still be regarded as pristine. The magnificent trees reached great heights. They grew in dense groves but with a fairly open understory. Inside the groves it was cool and redolent with scents of resin and fir needles. Within the groves open glades would appear suddenly as springs rose from the volcanic soil and carved runnels across grass grown marshy ground. Shade loving wild flowers circled the glades, sharing the space with ranked clumps of false helsbore. As a non-scientist, these aesthetic gifts were my chief reward for each visit. I could take the feelings away to last for a time in sensate memory in the more human influenced environment outside.

In the early 1980s a few scientists in their wisdom decided the forest had yielded enough of its secrets to research as an old growth site. It was time to allow some selective harvesting of the treasure. Let it be known that not all the scientists associated with the site agreed with this decision. They thought perhaps not all the questions had been answered. They thought perhaps new questions would arise over time. And they thought less invasive, less drastic approaches should be used than the ones which were chosen.

Foresters have developed many new approaches to logging since acknowledging the often disastrous results of an all over approach such as clear cutting. Environmental and ecological factors are now considered in the development of new harvesting techniques. These can range from a method leaving a few seed trees per acre to a range of selective cutting of carefully chosen trees. The characteristics and projected longevity of the 'leave trees' are important factors. Soil health, projected natural regeneration and local climate conditions are all factors vital in the design of a cutting program.

The harvest plan chosen for the part of the experimental forest to be cut would leave about five seed trees per acre. The areas chosen for cutting began at the mid level elevation of the mountain and ranged to its crest. The cut areas were on the south facing slope. The cut areas were largely adjacent, resulting in a large area of greatly diminished vegetation with sharply defined edges where the natural forest met the newly cut areas. Justifications for the choice were not only that the old growth forest had yielded all its research information, but that the harvested areas would provide new research opportunities.

I saw the forest in the early 1980s soon after the logging had commenced. I had not visited in a few years and fought hard to retain my old memories of the place. I also tried hard to acknowledge and accept the need for wood in our society. After all, I myself preferred my wooden house with its redwood paneling and wooden deck to a stucco version. But I found it difficult to accept the notion that this one forest could not be kept in its natural state, that somehow the wood from this small location was needed to supply the national needs. That the scientific inquiries, past and future, provided by the forest could not be reason enough to keep it in its natural state. That the research to be provided by its cut-over condition could not be found in any of a thousand commercially cut sites.

On the second post-logging visit there was evidence of plans gone awry. A standard practice after logging was to pile and burn the slash left after the cut was completed and the timber removed. This measure reduced both future fire danger and the possibility of massive invasion of the slash, and consequently the remaining trees, by insects. Both practices have the best of intentions when practiced with caution. In this case the piles of slash had been too high, too close to the remaining trees, the burn day was too warm, or all of the above. The fire had gotten away from the tenders and irrevocably damaged the remaining seed trees in many of the cut over areas at the lower elevations. The regenerative ability of the sites was destroyed. In the following fifteen years white thorn brush was to be practically the only plant to take root in the burned over areas. Tall charred and whitened spars would rise skyward through the impenetrable brush, sole testament to the former presence of a healthy forest. Score minus one for theoretical science in the service of economic pressure.

The other day I visited the forest again for the first time in several years. I had been warned about what I would see but even the warning was not sufficient to prevent my shocked reaction. In the unburned logged areas on the south slope of the mountain a scene of utter devastation prevailed.

Early last winter there was a wind storm of gigantic proportions which wreaked havoc over much of northern California. Trees and electrical transmission towers were blown down in numerous areas and the power was out for several days in much of that part of the state. As spring came and access to winter isolated areas became possible, the extent of the storm became evident. Broken and uprooted trees showed just where the violent winds had reached.

At the experimental forest the winds must have hit with incredible force on the southern slopes of the mountain. The sparse remaining tree cover was subject to the full power of the storm on that weather exposed site. In northern California the storms come in from that direction, it is the weather side of any location. In the more exposed areas three quarters of the trees were down, uprooted or snapped off by the winds. Like lightening attracted to the highest point, the gusts seem to have chosen the tallest most robust trees.

Trunks up to four feet in diameter covered the ground like a giant's abandoned game of pick up sticks. Shattered stubs of broken off trees rose in jagged testament to the power of the storm. Many of the few remaining standing trees had lost their tops. It was the smaller trees which survived. The giants lay on the ground in an incomprehensible jumbled mass. I could only marvel at the imagined scene during the fury of the storm. There would have been no safe haven.

The thought that this must have been a 'hundred year' storm was immediately chased away by the recollection of two other such storms in the thirty years of my acquaintance with this region. This was not the rarity it seemed at first notice. It could occur again. For the site at hand the damage is now complete.

There will be no natural regeneration. In point of fact new growth was not occurring even in the unburned areas, there were few visible young trees. The hand of man having intervened to the extent it had, it would now be necessary to humanly induce a new forest, by hand planting. Second guessing nature had not paid off.

The downed logs were already marked for cut and removal. It would provide an unexpected bonus in the projected cut of this area for the year. Once removed there would be slash and burning to deal with once more. While humans were dealing promptly with the situation, I could not view it as other than an avertable event.

In my despair at what I was viewing, I searched for reasons, explanations, the assurance that we can prevent in the future the possibility of such waste and destruction. In addition to the different ways this situation could have been handled, I found myself thinking of a managed working oak forest I had visited in the Loire region of central France. The management plan there has a two hundred forty year cycle. Trees being harvested now were saplings in Napoleon's time. The saplings of today will be harvested in the 2190s. Over the two hundred forty year span of human care and nurturing the trees will be thinned and limbed thirty five times. All for the benefit of any given caretaker's descendants eight generations in the future. Is it not time we took a similar long view before the possibilities of doing so escape us? Must a moment of greed and the conviction that we have all the answers obtainable from an environment lead us to the loss of humility at the wonder of a natural setting untouched by the hand of man? There is ample evidence that such attitudes can lead to irrevocable destruction.

Slender Green Strands

The banks of the mountain creek are lush with lupines and yellow daisies where it tumbles through a narrow green meadow. Behind their thirsty ranks grow wild orchids, magenta paintbrush and purple asters. Where the soil is rich, grass and scattered flowers grow twenty yards out on each side of the stream, forming a band of green in the rocky volcanic landscape. Where the dry volcanic soil encroaches to the creek side, a dusty silver foliaged lupine, smaller and less intensely purple, has adapted to the drier site.

Is it the wisdom of age which allows me to revel in the slender strand of green, appreciating each of its flora and enjoying the contrast with the rocky forested slopes around? I can remember being younger and wishing that a meadow like this would sweep away to the horizon, soothing my eye with green. Now the very contrast it provides seems to make me appreciate it more. I've grown to value contrasts in all their variety, each part gaining added interest by its very difference from the other.

I believe that I have learned to appreciate the arid western landscape in its entirety in the same way I can now value that slender green meadow in the otherwise dry landscape of the high mountain park. I can remember feeling almost threatened by aridity. Deserts were especially oppressive. I used to examine each new environ with an eye to what living there would be like. The habit no doubt arose from a nomadic childhood on three continents. It was a technique needed to survive emotionally in each new place. And to a child's mind any place might be the new place one had to live. This 'what if I lived here' approach can be enjoyed but needn't be applied to every landscape. Some don't need me or any other humans, they should be left untouched. My nomadic past has changed to a system of travel from a home base. It has given me new ways to enjoy the landscape.

Looking at a new landscape with an eye to the natural wonder, the adaptation of sister animal species and the plant world, is fascination enough in many cases. And the eye itself can find satisfaction and excitement in color, form and shape.

Even the driest, plant sparse desert can hold interest when looked at this way. I don't need to imagine living everywhere. I can choose one place I like and appreciate the others for their variety and diversity.

The contrast of edges is perhaps an experience gained by a more accepting view of varied landscapes. There is an excitement to edges not found in the limited viewscape of a more uniform environment. Experiencing the narrow green meadow allows an intimacy not possible in an environment stretching to the horizon in uniformity.

One of our contemporary Western authors who writes with great concern for the environment said that he thought perhaps the things he loved best about the West were there because of the aridity. Some of the historical responses to aridity he decried as he came to understand the natural landscape of the West. With maturity I too can take a new view of the arid western landscape. I needn't imagine expanding the narrow band of a mountain meadow to the edges of my viewed horizon. Changing the land to suit a preconceived ideal of satisfying lushness, even in the mind's eye, is not desirable. It takes away the pleasure to be seen in the local environment as it has evolved to fit the place at hand. It allows no appreciation of contrasts.

In country where water is limited, you must keep your eyes open, searching for the slender strands of green tucked in pockets of the landscape. Their value, to soothe the eye, cool the skin, or quench thirst, is doubly appreciated for their scarcity.

Fading Green

Beneath the hazed blue of a June skybowl

lush green fades to sered yellow-brown,

until it crumbles to chaff at a breath of wind.

Water robbed, life stripped, only dust remains.

Thinly clasping living green, a spring,

a stream in slender strands,

clings to water, life source of green.

Parceling moisture by precious drops

in a fading green band to crisp yellow borders,

Where the ghosts of spring grasses

rustle beneath the hazy sky.

Lost Creek

A covering gray cloud sits low on the mountain circled horizon.

Down one arc an ancient lava flow, tree covered at its mountain end,

fades sparse to greenness over purpled black talus patches.

The mountain arc bumps irregularly north,

undulating timbered ridges pierced by snow capped peaks.

In the circled valley lava fingers define zones of contrast.

Lush greenness follows one creek,

pines and firs trailing meadow edges.

Another stays hidden, a secret stream.

Where lava fingers palm to barren dryness,

a surprise of flowing water alternates in jumping riffles and languid pools

through jumbled outcrops of upthrust lava.

A tangle of dryland brush and the occasional gray fire scarred snag

meet willows and grass footed at the creek's narrow bank,

a thin trickle of living green through the brown rock barrens.

In late spring the rocky earth blooms with a wonderment of bright flowers,

their contrast causing one to suppose

they've only blown in on the wind,

somehow not belonging

to the dry brushy bowl of the lava barrens.

Life Cycle

Two momentous heart touching events occurred in our lives last summer. An already cherished grandchild was born. And a long cherished but lost-to-alcohol brother returned to a conscious life in the family circle. That event occurred on a Sunday. Our granddaughter was born the next day. We were present at both events. Our emotional cup ran over. And we were exhausted, at once drained and filled.

It was a four day roller coaster ride of emotions. Friday we learned that our over-due grandchild would be born by Caesarian section the following Monday morning. We were excited that we could definitely be present, making the three hour drive well before the planned moment.

Saturday we met with our interventionist to rehearse the unannounced intervention, planned for Sunday, to confront my brother with his alcoholism and try to get him into treatment. Daughters, brother and sister, sister-in-law and brother-in-law, nephews, niece, a friend, all came together in hopes of retrieving a person lost to us. We cried our way through reading the letters we had each written. They contained our anger, rage, frustration, sadness and longing for his old self, the one we all missed. Secrets came out, adults felt dismay at not having known the needs of emotionally abandoned nieces. Childhood memories cheered and saddened at the same time. A friend's observations confirmed our determination to press ahead. Weeping and drained, we still felt a new closeness, a tightening of the family circle.

Sunday we arrived unannounced at my brother's house, before the first drink of the day was consumed. Guided by our interventionist, we read our letters aloud to him. Choking, voices catching, but with fewer tears than the day before, we were determined now. Caught off guard by our presence, overwhelmed by the tough love flowing through the room, my brother agreed to treatment. Giving him no time for second thoughts, the interventionist had arranged a month in a local live-in rehabilitation facility. We helped him pack. Daughters, brother and sister, drove him there. Arrangements made, we left him, like a freshman at the college dorm.

Back to an afternoon of recapitulations, assurances. We had done the right thing, it looked like it was going to work. We predicted he would get to love the place, it would be his new addiction. That's pretty much the way it worked out, he didn't want to leave at the end of the month. AA is now his new addiction, and his salvation.

Early Monday morning we drove to the hospital where our granddaughter was to be born. Within minutes of her birth she was brought to a room where we waited with our co-grandparents. All first time grandparents, we reveled in holding that small perpetuation of our lives. The life cycle was renewing itself. In two days we had been witness to both the start of a new life and the renewal of an older one.

The second morning of her life our granddaughter showed her interest in the natural world. To allow his exhausted wife a few moments of rest, our son took his fussing daughter out into the cool of an early Central Valley summer morning. He stood with her to watch branches waving in the gentle breeze and to appreciate the wonder of her small life in his arms. Her day old eyes caught the movement of leaves. Watching, feeling the gentle breeze, she grew calm.

My brother is a keen observer of the natural world. He loves both the larger picture and the small-patch-of-the-earth viewpoints. Somewhere in the alcohol years even those pleasures were lost. He can now look forward to recapturing those interests.

We look forward to visits from both. Perhaps together, great niece and great uncle can explore the pleasures of our country place. They can watch the creek, look for wildflowers, see the gray squirrels chattering about their business, enjoy the wind in the trees. For one the experience will be all wondrously new. For the other it will be a renewal, a reappreciation of the natural world so long left behind in a miasma of alcohol filled urgencies.

The Comet

I saw a visitor tonight, ten million miles afar.

Below the steady dipper's handle, a soft white blur.

Seven miles of pulsing star dust winked across space leagues.

Behind the moon's dark void it spread its glowing tail.

Fifteen thousand years before return,

Who will see its journey then?

In space time it has often traveled here,

In human time I am awed to be its viewer.

The Feel of a Place

It is a strange but fairly common experience to be suddenly reminded of a place by an unexpected aroma. With no thoughts of a particular time or place in your head, the smell of a flower, or food cooking, or the very scents in the wind can take your consciousness to a time or place in the past. While usually explainable upon reflection, it is still a surprising sensation.

Visual similarities between widely disparate places are common as well. And usually they are intellectually explainable. A wet meadow with stunted conifers on the slopes of Mt. Shasta in northern California always reminded me of Alaska, even before I had been to that state. When I did visit Alaska the muskeg meadows of the central part of the state did indeed resemble the familiar meadow in California.

While traveling in New Zealand I often had the sensation of being in coastal northern California. Then a tree fern would come into view and destroy the sensation. But the grassy brush covered hills and the great forests of Monterey pine, imported of course from California, when seen out of context could put my mind somewhere near home.

Far from lessening the pleasure of seeing a new environment, these familiar connections tend to make the world seem smaller. They make a comfortable connection with the more intimate surroundings of home. They form a bridge between disparate areas. But they leave the differences between diverse places as noticeable and intact contrasts. There are no low bush cranberries or blueberries in that Mt. Shasta meadow. Tree ferns do not grow on the hills of coastal California.

I have recently experienced what for me is a new form of reminder of previously known places. Completely unbidden, with no overt visual or aromatic clues, I have been reminded of places well known in my childhood. Each time the stimulant has been so radically different that it has taken me some time to discern the reason for the memory jog. That search is not without its pleasures but at times I am amazed at the slim connection unearthed.

A few years ago I was commuting to some classes at a local university about seventy miles distant from my home. About half the trip was by back country roads, little traveled by others. Admittedly, I was able to go into a sort of autopilot mode on some stretches and enjoy the leisure of wandering thoughts. After the first few trips I became aware that at a certain spot in each journey I always thought of a road between two mountain villages in rural Japan where I had often walked as a teenager. I had never driven an automobile on that particular Asian road, but each time the car came to a certain curve on a down slope of the northern California highway I was reminded of the Japanese country road. There were no visual similarities at all. The vegetation was entirely different. There were no villages or even buildings on the California highway. The only similarity must have been the exact curve, slope and length of the two roads, I can imagine no other reason for the memories. In my mind the spot has now become known as the "Furuma curve", named for one of the villages in Japan.

On a research trip to Mexico, we stopped in a small rural town in the state of Michoacan to meet with some local officials. As we entered the narrow streets with their red tile roofed, whitewashed, adobe walled houses, I began recalling travels through small towns in rural Japan. Again the visual similarities were so few as to be incomparable. The people of course looked nothing alike. The Japanese buildings would have been built of white plaster and wood with black tile roofs. It can only have been the narrow dirt streets with houses and stores opening right off the thoroughfares, the views of dark interiors through wide front openings, and glimpses of light filled interior courtyards or gardens seen through many rooms which jogged the memory. There were also few vehicles, just the occasional cart and many pedestrians pursuing their errands on foot. Like the curve in the road, I can best attribute the occurrence of the memories to the feel of the place.

A similar surprising memory occurred in the Loire region of central France. I was privileged to live for three months in a suburban town near Orleans which had been in previous centuries a resort area for the nearby city. The wealthiest city citizens built chateaux in park like settings along the tiny Loiret River. The less affluent but still wealthy merchant classes had built smaller houses with tiny walled gardens along some stretches of the same river. Narrow dirt streets lined these neighborhoods. Occasional paths led down to the river bank for limited public access to the water. The Tokyo neighborhoods of my youth had only channeled rivers and frequent odoriferous canals but the narrow roads and walled houses were similar enough in sensate memory to trigger there in the alleys along the Loiret, sharp memories of a very different place.

Each of these episodes of recall has been a surprise and a mystery. And yet each has made me thankful for the memory of a long unseen place, places which would no doubt be very different if I were able to return today. I find myself eagerly awaiting the next such episode, some of these places seem almost unrecallable otherwise. Each time the pleasure of a revisit in sensate memory is acute. And I seem unable to experience them with quite the same intensity in any other way.

Traces Left Behind

There'll be a small trace of me that I'll leave behind after eight years in this area. Quite literally. Actually, I'm not sure about the ultimate disposal of biohazardous materials. Maybe they end up somewhere in the Mojave Desert. Or up in smoke. Probably either alternative is better than my vision of a tiny burial site for the disfunctional gall bladder which I have gladly given up.

The gall bladder, a useful little storage sac for extra bile, depicted in a bilious green color (pun fully intended) on the digestive system charts in the doctor's office, is a body piece you're quite willing to part with if it becomes filled with stones of its own making. A little bag of various sized marbles, it may be unnoticeable until the smallest ones begin moving down ducts to other parts of the body. Backache, spasms, heartburn, these announce that it's time to do something about the stones.

Not quite as useless as the appendix, when removed the gall bladder's functions will be taken over by the liver and one can return to a blissful state of normalcy in diet and regimen. Altogether not a part to be mourned when it is in a stone making mode. And since the surgeon had pronounced me a "well developed and well nurtured mature female" with no "signs of distress", I was eager to be rid of the offending marbles.

I did wonder about the doctor's description of me. Was the reference to the body or the mind? Were my one hundred forty five pounds spread over a five foot eight inch frame the reason for the phrase "well developed and well nurtured"? We had had a far ranging fairly intellectual question and answer session. I prefer to think the reference included the mind as well as the overall size of the body. Even though the doctor was probably only an inch or two taller than I am.

Though I joyfully parted from my little sac of marbles, I do wonder where it is. Somehow the indignity of a mass gravesite with other biohazardous materials doesn't satisfy the romantic mindset. I'd like to think of it buried deep in pine needle duff in the center of an old stand of Ponderosa pine with a splashing creek singing nearby. The idea of the Mojave won't do. The smoke and ashes are probably a truer possibility and more acceptable. The ashes could settle over my imaginary grove and drift to the ground to be recycled as part of the natural scene. A suitable alternative to a miniature burial site.

Rediscovery

Summer is the time I know the best in this area. Eight years of living here year round, plus the twelve earlier summers we spent in the area, add up to sixty months of summer explorations. Perhaps it's the earlier associations of summertime, but winters here almost make me feel like this is a different place rather than a logical progression of the seasons in one location.

In spite of the familiarity and accompanying fond remembrances, the last summer of our residence has invoked as much boredom as nostalgia. We know there are places we want to visit and experience again, know we'll even enjoy them intensely, but the motivation to go is somehow lacking. We're bored with all the old places, we regretfully admit to each other. We feel limited by the very fact of familiarity. We are ready for new explorations, new experiences.

To our surprise, we have found both in the course of revisiting old haunts. A fifteen mile loop road we'd never taken beckons and rewards with views of old growth forest around the site of an old summer home tract. The aging cabins fit the mold of how summer places should look, wooden shelters for stolen weekends away from the city. Here are no gravel yards with maintenance free plants around stucco houses which could serve as full time homes. I suspect the cabin kitchens are barely functional, the bathrooms sport no jacuzzi tubs, the walls are uninsulated. Life seems to be lived mostly on the large decks adjacent to each cabin.

We discover the joys of swimming in the cool shallows of one of the mountain lakes in the nearby national park. We wonder why we never swam there before. We go off trail and wander beside the streams lacing the nearby mountain meadows. Mellifluous water sounds lead us in curves and loops to tiny gardens of streamside wildflowers whose names we pursue in our flower identification handbook. There are new things to discover even in old familiar places.

That old friend nostalgia is also eagerly welcomed at unexpected moments. A hot midday breeze stirring the pines where I sit reading brings visions of past camping trips and afternoon laziness beneath the open flaps of a tent. Nostalgia is a welcome guest in the search for remembrances.

At a spring filled meadow we rediscover a spot unvisited for over twenty years. We find it bravely recovered from that last visit when the scars of fresh logging ruined our previous remembrance of lush mossy banks of the rocky stream emerging full blast from spring laced cliffs. A wide variety of plants not abundantly found in this region have returned to crowd the shores of the stream. Luxuriant mosses cover the creek banks and midstream boulders, sedges and horsetail crowd the moist banks. Mountain ash and elderberry sport heavy berry crops, wild azaleas are everywhere. It must be beautiful in early summer with the heady scent of the white azaleas and the vibrant red slashes of the blooms of leopard lilies and columbine dipping above the water.

I find myself thinking of returning another summer. Maybe I should not think of this summer as a time of last visits but simply a time of rediscovery and affirmation of the pleasures of this mountain region. Perhaps rediscovery can carry equal weight with the excitement of new explorations and experiences.

The Hike to No Name Lake

At road's end the smell of fir duff,

thick from fallen needles of old growth giants,

sets the senses for a walk up a little touched valley.

Signs announce a human boundary, and eighty year old blazes,

hatchet wide and inches buried in dense grown bark,

show beside the faint trail.

Beyond those human incursions the four and five foot

trunks of pine and fir show a world

as first explorers must have found it.

Cabin sized boulders fallen from the palisaded heights

in some primordial era, stand surrounded by tall guardian firs

which sheltered in their lee as tiny saplings.

The occasional boulder sustains a shallow growth on top and sides;

flowers, moss, and tiny offspring of the guardian giants make high

miniature gardens.

Meadows ranked with corn lilies flow beneath the feet of aspens grown to great

height

beside the stream cascading from the hidden valley above.

Climbing the ridge the forest thickens darkly to a stand of pure fir

with only the occasional company of a brilliant crimson shaft of snow plant

emerging from the deep duff covered ground.

The rocky ridge crests at the hidden valley's lip,

notched only for the passage of the crashing stream

to fall frothing to the forest floor below.

In infinite perfection the valley opens in the strong embrace of pillared cliffs,

a cirque of eroding stone and talus slope around three sides.

Whitely frothed snow melt cascades down an avalanche slope

to fill the deep bowl of a green moraine lake.

Meadows thick with grass and wandering streams crisscross the slope below,

burying in green the scattered firs lying torn and twisted by the latest

winter avalanche.

On the clear lake surface water boatmen hop and skip,

their miniature motions reflected on the silty bottom

as concentric overlapping circles in a dance of light.

The dull roar of the cascades plunging down the talus slope is pierced

by the thin call of migrating birds foraging in stream side willow groves.

Supine in the tall grass, a hat brim view of the rim above

reveals the wraith like forms of early afternoon clouds;

wispy dragons and mythical beasts precede gathering cumuli

in an effervescent dance on a cliff top stage.

High above the ethereal blue bowl sports drifting continents

of ephemerality in an ever changing map.

Winding Up

Ten months to go. We can actually count days, mark off blocks on a calendar. It is both soothing and disturbing. I worry that this attitude will make me unappreciative of the present, that I'll just be marking time.

In ten months my husband will retire and we will return to our home in the Bay Area after an eight year hiatus. It is an event we have looked forward to for all of those eight years. Looked forward to but rarely allowed ourselves to think about. It was a vague rosy plan for the future, nothing more. If we had let it be more, had begun counting days when there were three thousand to go, we would have lived in perpetual frustration. Now suddenly there seems no reason to push the idea aside. In fact we need to think about it, we need to make plans. We need to wind up our sojourn in this rural area.

Before the pleasure of returning home can take place there is a series of nasty annoying practical things to be done. None of them can be termed pleasurable. They are the price to be paid for getting something desirable at the end. Getting the property ready to sell, putting it on the market, dealing with potential buyers, all these things can overwhelm if I allow them to. And after those hurdles there will be the actual task of moving. I get tired just thinking about it.

And what of the eight year hiatus? How did we approach that period? I guess mostly by trying to regard the whole time as a vacation of sorts. We were in the mountains, in a rural area. We had a beautiful piece of property with tall forest and a year round creek. In summer it was like going camping but getting to sleep in a real bed. In winter the house took on the feel of a ski cabin, especially when the snow reached our elevation. Doesn't sound so bad? Really it was less than bad, it had its pleasurable times.

But home continued to pull. Home is so much more than the spot where all one's possessions are collected. It's people, family, familiarity, an ease and contentment with the surroundings. If we're lucky, it's a place where roots run deep. I couldn't even bring myself to call the country place home until well into the fifth year. Even as I said it a small flag would pop up in my mind, a qualifier about what was really home. I almost felt disloyal using the word 'home' about the place where I knew I would not stay, the place where my roots were shallow.

The winding up process is strange. Rather like the last few days of a vacation. Mentally you are preparing to leave, to return home. You don't take in sights and sensations the way you do at the start of a journey when everything is fresh and exciting. Now we make less of an effort to explore, to make new friends, to forge connections. My husband is doubly affected, he is winding up a long career. He is less of a player at the office, often not consulted on long range plans or new research projects. He won't be around when they happen. Intellectually these things were anticipated, they're just having a greater impact than expected. And unlike those last few days of a vacation this experience is stretching out over a period of months. Maybe it's just as well we'll be so busy with those nasty annoying practical details, there'll be less time to contemplate the strange tugs of the wrap-up period.

The View From Home

The movements and actions are all so automatic that it amazes me. In spite of an eight year hiatus of living in another house the patterns and paths of this house are ingrained in my mind. Getting up in the morning I trace a path without thinking, reaching for clothes where they hang on the door, opening curtains, going out for the paper. Sometimes I even reach for something that isn't there anymore, something we have moved or gotten rid of altogether.

We've returned to a house we left eight years ago. Moving back in, we had a tendency to put things in their old places. It made the unpacking and rearranging a fairly easy task. But newly acquired things had to wait to be put away until the old objects found their accustomed spots. The old objects seemed to have priority rights. If we changed the location of something it would throw us off base, we wouldn't know where to look for it. There were times when one of us couldn't remember where we had kept something when we lived in the house before. If we asked the other one though, they usually remembered. "Where did we keep the spare batteries before?" I asked as I searched for a logical place. "There was a gray cardboard file box on the shelf over the washing machine, remember?" Of course. A picture of the very box came immediately to mind. The batteries returned to their old spot but in a new box, we didn't seem to have the old gray one anymore.

Setting up the kitchen was a particularly challenging experience. If I thought about it I really couldn't remember where a lot of things had been kept. But if I just put them out on the counter and stood there as if putting them away after having washed up, my mind off somewhere else, they went magically into their old places. The problems arose when it came to anything that was recently acquired. I had to find new spots for those items and I still have trouble finding them when I need to use them.

And then there were the two rooms which previously had been the domains of our children. They were open to completely new arrangements. It was decidedly an easier task arranging them since we didn't have to remove the signs of their previous occupancy, those had been stripped away when we prepared to rent out the house. There were memories attached to the spaces but we were free to organize them to fit our present needs. Setting up those two rooms was like moving into a new house. Consequently they don't hold the same ingrained patterns that the other rooms do. We like their new incarnations as study and studio but they are also the prime locations for all lost objects, we're just not familiar with the contents of either room yet.

The things that amuse and amaze me the most about returning to a house we lived in before are those that give evidence of the old ingrained habits. Changing my clothes in the bedroom the other day, I instinctively began to throw the dirty clothes down to my right on the closet floor. The clothes hamper stood right in front of me, I was staring at it, wondering why I felt like throwing the dirty clothes on the floor. I am not a dirty clothes on the floor person. I stopped myself in mid throw, remembering that we used to keep a dirty clothes basket on the floor of the closet. It was probably in that spot for fifteen years before we moved. The motion was so built into my brain that as I stood in that familiar spot it seemed the natural thing to do to take off the dirty clothes and toss them in that now non-existent basket.

We used to keep a dish towel on the cabinet door under the kitchen sink. When we moved back we decided on a new location for the towel, easier to reach and to avoid having a wet towel hanging on the door. But I still reach down instinctively with wet drippy hands to find the towel on the door, even if I happen to be looking at the one hanging in its new spot.

If there is something new I'm looking for that had no previous life in this house, or if we changed the location of something old when we returned, I have a terrible time finding it. In spite of all the logic that went into deciding where things would be stored I sometimes have to search for ten minutes in several rooms before finding the object. When we moved away I could remember exactly where each thing had been stored in this house. Now the problem is that I can remember where it was stored in the intervening house as well as where it was in this house before that. My mind takes me through both places, then I try to rely on the logic which rearranged this house when we returned. If all these tactics fail, the hunt is on and every cabinet, drawer and closet is searched before the sought after object is finally located in its perfectly logical new spot.

So the house is both old and new, a repository of memories which come flooding unbidden out of the simplest places or the most ordinary actions and at the same time it is an adventurous new place creating new habits and associations. Both aspects of the house are pleasant, the familiarity and the newness. Just a bit frustrating when you really do need to find the light bulbs.

About the Author

Sidney Oltman Ferrell was born to American parents in Tokyo Japan. She was educated at the American School in Japan and received her bachelor's degree from Swarthmore College in Pennsylvania. She has also lived in Colombia, Canada and France. She is an author and a fiber artist. She founded a textile business, St. Clair Designs, which specialized in the design and production of custom rugs and fabrics for the interior design market. Her artworks in weaving, basketry and handmade paper have been shown in exhibitions throughout the U.S. and are found in several private collections.

0-595-30212-2

1

www.ingramcontent.com/pod-product-compliance
Lightning Source LLC
Chambersburg PA
CBHW061303280526
45784CB00002B/872